POINT NO POINT

Also by Sujata Bhatt from Carcanet

Brunizem
Monkey Shadows
The Stinking Rose

Sujata Bhatt

POINT NO POINT

Selected Poems

CARCANET

First published in 1997 by
Carcanet Press Limited
4th Floor, Conavon Court
12-16 Blackfriars Street
Manchester M3 5BQ

A CIP catalogue record for this book
is available from the British Library
ISBN 1 85754 306 8

The publisher acknowledges financial assistance
from the Arts Council of England

Set in 10pt Palatino by Bryan Williamson, Frome
Printed and bound in England by SRP Ltd, Exeter

for

Michael and Jenny Mira

Contents

Point No Point

Why name a place Point No Point?

Does it mean we are nowhere
when we reach it?

Does it mean we lose our sense
of meaning, our sense of direction
when we stop at Point No Point?

Begin again, add
that it was the place we almost missed,
and then it was the place we returned to
                                    again and again
braking at the abrupt dirt road detour –

Hidden by trees, entangled
                        in disagreements,
        we found shelter, a view –
a clearing that was not a clearing.

Why name a place Point No Point?
In any case, here we are, you said,
in a new landscape – will it change your mind?
Here we are
in a game called 'begin at zero' –
how many lighthouses can you love
without fainting?
And can you find enough
pine trees to define the infinite dark green?
If zero is love on the way to the lighthouse
then where is the balance?
And will it change your mind?
Will the sky provide a clue to your confusion?

Well, here we are, you said, now try
to understand the Juan de Fuca Strait.

Begin again, remember
once we stopped for no reason,
back-tracked down to Point No Point
for no reason except that the light
was sudden – it pulled us in,
          kept us still.

Then, just when we thought it was time
to leave, we saw them:
a group of orcas in the distance – seven,
maybe eight – they were swimming towards us –

black and white, and black and white
their rising and falling: generous, endless
                    black and white, they burned –
it was their bodies that made
                    the waves alert –
it was the largeness of their yearning, an innocent
                   violence spinning within their grace –
black and white, and black and white
the surface: muscular, turbulent – It was more
than passion,   more
                                          that made our blood learn –

that made our blood learn.

from

BRUNIZEM

Sujata: The First Disciple of Buddha

One morning, a tall lean man
stumbled towards me.
His large eyes: half closed
as if he were seasick;
his thick black hair full of dead leaves and bumble-bees
grew wild as weeds and fell way below his hips.
His beard swayed gently as an elephant's trunk.
'I'm hungry,' he muttered.
I took him home, fed him fresh yoghurt and bread.
Then, I bathed him, shaved his face clean and smooth,
coconut oiled his skin soft again.
It took four hours
to wash and comb his long hair,
which he refused to cut.
For four hours he bent his head this way and that
while I ploughed through his hair
with coconut oil on my fingers.
'And *how* did you get this way?' I asked.
'I haven't slept for years,' he said.
'I've been thinking, just thinking.
I couldn't sleep or eat
until I had finished thinking.'
After the last knot
had been pulled out of his hair, he slept,
still holding on to my sore fingers.
The next morning, before the sun rose,
before my father could stop me,
he led me to the wide-trunked, thick-leafed bodhi tree
to the shady spot where he had sat for years
and asked me to listen.

The Peacock

His loud sharp call
seems to come from nowhere.
Then, a flash of turquoise
        in the pipal tree.
The slender neck arched away from you
          as he descends,
and as he darts away, a glimpse
        of the very end of his tail.

I was told
that you have to sit in the veranda
                    and read a book,
preferably one of your favourites
        with great concentration.
The moment you begin to live
inside the book
a blue shadow will fall over you.
The wind will change direction,
the steady hum of bees
in the bushes nearby
will stop.
The cat will awaken and stretch.
Something has broken your attention;
and if you look up in time
you might see the peacock
turning away as he gathers in his tail
to shut those dark glowing eyes,
violet fringed with golden amber.
It is the tail that has to blink
for eyes that are always open.

Iris

Her hand sweeps over the rough grained paper,
then, with a wet sponge, again.
A drop of black is washed grey,
cloudy as warm breath fogging cool glass.
She feels she must make the best of it,
she must get the colour of the stone wall,
of the mist settling around twisted birch trees.
Her eye doesn't miss the rabbit crouched,
a tuft of fog in the tall grass.
Nothing to stop the grey sky from merging into stones,
or the stone walls from trailing off into sky.
But closer, a single iris stands fully opened:
dark wrinkled petals, rain-moist,
the tall slender stalk sways, her hand follows.
Today, even the green is tinged with grey,
the stone's shadow lies heavy over the curling petals
but there's time enough, she'll wait,
study the lopsided shape.
The outer green sepals once enclosing the bud
lie shrivelled: empty shells spiralling
right beneath the petals.
As she stares the sun comes out.
And the largest petal flushes
deep deep violet.
A violet so intense it's almost black.
The others tremble indigo, reveal
paler blue undersides.
Thin red veins running into yellow orange rills,
yellow flows down the green stem.
Her hand moves swiftly from palette to paper,
paper to palette, the delicate brush
swoops down, sweeps up,
moves the way a bird builds its nest.
An instant and the sun is gone.
Grey-ash-soft-shadows fall again.
But she can close her eyes and see

red-orange veins, the yellow
swept with green throbbing towards blue,
and deep inside she feels
indigo pulsing to violet.

ઉડેલી *(Udaylee)*

Only paper and wood are safe
from a menstruating woman's touch.
So they built this room
for us, next to the cowshed.
Here, we're permitted to write
letters, to read, and it gives a chance
for our kitchen-scarred fingers to heal.

Tonight, I can't leave the stars alone.
And when I can't sleep, I pace
in this small room, I pace
from my narrow rope-bed to the bookshelf
filled with dusty newspapers
held down with glossy brown cowries and a conch.
When I can't sleep, I hold
the conch shell to my ear
just to hear my blood rushing,
a song throbbing,
a slow drumming within my head, my hips.
This aching is my blood flowing against,
rushing against something –
knotted clumps of my blood,
so I remember fistfuls of torn seaweed
        rising with the foam,
rising. Then falling, falling up on the sand
strewn over newly laid turtle eggs.

The Doors Are Always Open

Everywhere you turn there are goats,
some black and lumpy.
Others, with oily mushroom-soft hair,
sticky yellow in Muslim sand
shaded by the mosque.
Next door
there's a kerosene smeared kitchen.
We share a window
with the woman who lives with goats.
Now she unwraps some cheese
now she beats and kneads
a little boy   and screams
'Idiot! Don't you tease that pregnant goat again!'
I look away: outside
the rooster runs away
from his dangling sliced head
while the pregnant goat lies with mourning hens.
Her bleating consolations
make the children spill
cheesy milk and run outside.
Wet soccer ball bubbles roll out
from a hole beneath the lifted tail.
The goat licks her kids free,
pushing, pushing
until they all wobble about.
We've counted five.
Hopping up and down, we push each other
until we see
the goat pushing her kids
to stand up, until
mothers call us back
                    to thick milk.

શેરડી *(Shérdi)*

The way I learned
to eat sugar cane in Sanosra:
I use my teeth
to tear the outer hard *chaal*
then, bite off strips
of the white fibrous heart –
suck hard with my teeth, press down
and the juice spills out.

January mornings
the farmer cuts tender green sugar-cane
and brings it to our door.
Afternoons, when the elders are asleep
we sneak outside carrying the long smooth stalks.
The sun warms us, the dogs yawn,
our teeth grow strong
our jaws are numb;
for hours we suck out the *russ*, the juice
sticky all over our hands.

So tonight
when you tell me to use my teeth,
to such hard, harder,
then, I smell sugar cane grass
in your hair
and imagine you'd like to be
shérdi shérdi out in the fields
the stalks sway
opening a path before us

Swami Anand

In Kosbad during the monsoons
there are so many shades of green
your mind forgets other colours.

At that time
I am seventeen, and have just started
to wear a sari every day.
Swami Anand is eighty-nine
                    and almost blind.
His thick glasses don't seem to work,
they only magnify his cloudy eyes.
Mornings he summons me
      from the kitchen
and I read to him until lunch time.

One day he tells me
'you can read your poems now'
I read a few, he is silent.
Thinking he's asleep, I stop.
But he says, 'continue'.
I begin a long one
in which the Himalayas rise
                    as a metaphor.
Suddenly I am ashamed
to have used the Himalayas like this,
ashamed to speak of my imaginary mountains
to a man who walked through
          the ice and snow of Gangotri
                    barefoot
a man who lived close to Kangchenjanga
        and Everest clad only in summer cotton.
I pause to apologize
but he says 'just continue'.

Later, climbing through
        the slippery green hills of Kosbad,
Swami Anand does not need to lean
on my shoulder or his umbrella.
I prod him for suggestions,
ways to improve my poems.
He is silent a long while,
then, he says
        'there is nothing I can tell you
                except continue.'

For Nanabhai Bhatt

In this dream my grandfather
comes to comfort me.
He stands apart
silent
and in his face I see
the patience of his trees
on hot typhoid days
that promise no rain.

His eyes
the colour of a crow's feather in children's mud,
yet filled with sharp mountain-top light.

I'm sure this was the face the true bald man,
Gandhiji saw when he confessed
about the Harijan girl, the six-year-old
he adopted and tried to educate.
I'm sure these were the eyes the true hermaphrodite,
Gandhiji saw while he explained
how this girl cared too much for clothes,
how one day she went and had her hair bobbed,
the latest fashion, she said.
It was too much.
She had to be set straight,

the sooner the better.
So he had her head shaved
to teach her
not to look in mirrors so often.
At this point Gandhiji turned
towards my grandfather and allowed, so softly:
'But she cried.
I couldn't stop her crying.
She didn't touch dinner.
She cried all night.
I brought her to my room,
tucked her in my bed, sang her *bhajans*,
but she still cried.
I stayed awake beside her.

So this morning I can't think clearly,
I can't discuss our plans
for building schools in villages.'
And my grandfather
looked at him with the same face
he shows in my dream.

Muliebrity

I have thought so much about the girl
who gathered cow-dung in a wide, round basket
along the main road passing by our house
and the Radhavallabh temple in Maninagar.
I have thought so much about the way she
moved her hands and her waist
and the smell of cow-dung and road-dust and wet canna lilies,
the smell of monkey breath and freshly washed clothes
and the dust from crows' wings which smells different –
and again the smell of cow-dung as the girl scoops
it up, all these smells surrounding me separately
and simultaneously – I have thought so much
but have been unwilling to use her for a metaphor,

for a nice image – but most of all unwilling
to forget her or to explain to anyone the greatness
and the power glistening through her cheekbones
each time she found a particularly promising
mound of dung –

A Different History

Great Pan is not dead;
he simply emigrated
to India.
Here, the gods roam freely,
disguised as snakes or monkeys;
every tree is sacred
and it is a sin
to be rude to a book.
It is a sin to shove a book aside
with your foot,
a sin to slam books down
hard on a table,
a sin to toss one carelessly
across a room.
You must learn how to turn the pages gently
without disturbing Sarasvati,
without offending the tree
from whose wood the paper was made.

2

Which language
has not been the oppressor's tongue?
Which language
truly meant to murder someone?
And how does it happen

that after the torture,
after the soul has been cropped
with a long scythe swooping out
of the conqueror's face –
the unborn grandchildren
grow to love that strange language.

The Kama Sutra Retold

Then Roman Svirsky said,
'it is illegal in Russia to write
about sex
so it is important
for Vasily Aksyonov
to write about it –'

You laugh,
but I want to know
how would we break the long silence
if we had the same rules?

It's not enough to say
she kissed his balls,
licked his cock long
how her tongue could not stop.

For he thinks of the first day:
she turns her head away
as she takes off her T-shirt
blue jeans, underwear, bra.
She doesn't even look at him
until she's in the lake,
the clear water up to her neck
yet unable to hide her skin.

They swim out
to the islands
but he doesn't remember swimming;
just brushing against her leg
once, then diving down
beneath her thighs staying underwater
long enough for a good look,
coming up for air and watching
her black hair streaming back straight,
then watching her
step over
the stones, out of the water.

She doesn't know what to say.
He wishes they were swans.
Yeats's swans
would not need to speak
but could always glide across
other worlds;
magical, yet rustling with real reeds.

The sun in her eyes
so they move closer to the pine trees.
When he touches her nipples
he doesn't know
who is more surprised
(years later he remembers that look,
the way her eyes open wider).
He's surprised
she wants him
to kiss her nipples again and again
because she's only 17 he's surprised
her breasts are so full.
She's surprised
it feels so good
because he's only 17 she's surprised
he can be so gentle
yet so hard inside her,
the way pine needles
can soften the ground.
Where does the ground end

and she begin?
She must have swallowed the sky
the lake, and all the woods
veined with amber brown pathways;

for now great white wings
are swooping through
her thighs, beating stronger
up her chest,
the beak stroking her spine
feathers tingling her skin,
the blood inside
her groin swells

while wings are rushing to get out,
rushing.

Oranges and Lemons

The second time
I came alone to say
a farewell of sorts, I wanted one more
look at her handwriting.

I was prepared for solitude, a floating
amputated quietness circling my wrists –
but not this song, not this

Oranges and lemons
Sold for a penny
All the schoolgirls
Are so many . . .

They rush in breathless
climbing up behind me, ahead of me, up
the warehouse steep Dutch staircase
to Anne Frank's room.

Schoolgirls, mostly schoolgirls
ages 13-16, they whisper about the important
things – staring everywhere: at windows, corners,
the ceiling. Staring at the paper,
her patient paper, her brown ink.
And a few linger behind, preferring to squint through
the netting, as if expecting something to happen
down by the other houses, the trees –

The grass is green
The rose is red
Remember me
When I am dead . . .

And a few linger behind, whispering
about the important things.

The Women of Leh are such –

for Jürgen Dierking

The women of Leh are such –
that one night over there, some 3,600 metres
high, not far from Tibet,
where the Zanskar glitters all day,
and at night, the stars, not to be outdone,
seem to grow larger, let themselves sink down closer
to the mountains – while the moon always disappears
by midnight, cut off by the horizon,
always on the other side
of some huge rock – one night
in that place I dreamt
and I saw Gertrude Stein selling
horseradishes and carrots. There was no mistaking
those shoulders – but she fit in so well
with her looking-straight-at-you eyes.
And yet, even the traditional
Ladakhi hat she wore could not disguise

her face. She said *jooley* to my *jooley*
with the others, all lined up along the main street –
she slapped the head of a hungry
rowdily exploring *dzo*
and I walked back, several times, back and forth,
pretending I couldn't decide what to buy.
Then she turned aside to talk with the tomato seller,
still keeping an eye on the *dzo* – it was hard to believe
but there was no mistaking that poise.

What Is Worth Knowing?

That Van Gogh's ear, set free
wanted to meet the powerful nose
of Nevsky Avenue.
That Spain has decided to help
NATO. That Spring is supposed to begin
on the 21st of March.
That if you put too much salt in the *keema*
just add a few bananas.
That although the Dutch were the first
to help the people of Nicaragua they don't say much
about their history with Indonesia.
That Van Gogh collected Japanese prints.
That the Japanese considered
the Dutch to be red-haired barbarians.
That Van Gogh's ear remains full of questions
it wants to ask the nose of Nevsky Avenue.
That the vaccinations for cholera, typhoid and yellow fever
are no good – they must be improved.
That red, green and yellow are the most
auspicious colours.
That turmeric and chilli powder are good
disinfectants. Yellow and red.
That often Spring doesn't come
until May. But in some places
it's there in January.

That Van Gogh's ear left him because
it wanted to become a snail.
That east and west
meet only in the north and south – but never
in the east or west.
That in March 1986 Darwinism is being
reintroduced in American schools.
That there's a difference
between pigeons and doves, although
a ring-dove is a wood-pigeon.
That the most pleasant thing is to have a fever
of at least 101 – because then the dreams aren't
merely dreams but facts.
That during a fever the soul comes out
for fresh air, that during a fever the soul bothers to
speak to you.
That tigers are courageous and generous-hearted
and never attack unless provoked –
but leopards,
leopards are malicious and bad-tempered.
That buffaloes too,
water-buffaloes that is, have a short temper.
That a red sky at night is a good sign for sailors,
for sailors . . . what is worth knowing?
What is worth knowing?

Another Day in Iowa City

for Andrei Voznesensky

'My father's been to your country,' I begin.
But you interrupt, saying you want to go
to India . . . while I wonder
how your shirt is the same blue
as the blue dresses painted on
the glossy wooden Russian dolls
my father brought home one day.

Your shirt brought back
memories of my mother angry
at the government
for sending all our bananas to Russia.
Sturdy memories of Russian dolls and no bananas –
no bananas
but Russian dolls, one inside the other endlessly –
and the last doll, always my favourite,
a hard seed, a bright secret that would never open
although I could look through those small
small black eyes.

Tonight
how I focused on your shirt, your emphatic hands.
How I listened to you with snow falling, with snow
covering all the tired hoof-prints in my soul
I can not explain – and my noisy dreams
of Akaky Akakyvich searching for his overcoat
would make you laugh.

There's no way I could've told you
all this in public, in ten how-do-you-do minutes.

So later, when you paused to ask me:
'Don't you want to visit my country?'
with such questioning sadness –
I was ready to take off my shoes, ready to jump out
of the car, let's go, I wanted to say, let's go for a walk,
let's go for a swim, let's take the next flight out of here.

Hey,

your photographs
of Indian temples are incomplete.
Where's that man I saw every day
laughing
at the clean
Brahmin's children
who were afraid of him?
Where's that man
with the swollen elephant leg
who sits by the pillar
crawling with gods and flies?

Search For My Tongue

Days my tongue slips away.
I can't hold on to my tongue.
It's slippery like the lizard's tail
I try to grasp
but the lizard darts away.

મારી જીભ સરકી જાય છે
(mari jeebh sarki jai chay)
I can't speak. I speak nothing.
Nothing.

કાંઈ નહિ, હું નથી બોલી શકતી
(kai nahi, hoo nathi boli shakti)
I search for my tongue.

પરંતુ ક્યાં શોધું ? ક્યાં ?
(parantu kya shodhu? Kya?)

હું દોડતી દોડતી જાઉં છું.
(hoo dhodti dhodti jaoo choo)
But where should I start? Where?
I go running, running,

નદી કિનારે પ્હોચી છું, નદી કિનારે.
(nadi keenayray pohchee choo, nadi keenayray)
reach the river's edge.
Silence

એકદમ શાંત.
(akedum shant)

નીચે પાણી નહિ, ઉપ્પર પક્ષી નહિ.
(neechay pani nahi, oopur pakshi nahi)
Below, the riverbed is dry. Above,
the sky is empty: no clouds, no birds.
If there were leaves, or even grass
they would not stir today,
for there is no breeze.
If there were clouds
then, it might rain.

જો વાદળ હોત   તો કદાચ વરસાદ આવે,
(jo vadla hoat   toh kadach varsad aavay)

જો વરસાદ પડે તો નદી પાછી આવે.
(jo varsad puday toh nadi pachee aavay)

જો નદી હોય, જો પાણી હોય, તો કાંઇક લીલું લીલું દેખાય.
(jo nadi hoy, jo pani hoy, toh kaeek leelu leelu daykhai)
If the rains fell
then the river might return,
if the water rose again I might see something green
at first, then trees enough to fill a forest.
If there were some clouds that is.

જો વાદળા હોત તો.
(jo vadla hoat toh)
Since I have lost my tongue
I can only imagine
there is something crawling
beneath the rocks, now burrowing down
into the earth when I lift the rock.

જ્યારે પથ્થર ઉપાડું .
(jyaray patther oopadu)
The rock is in my hand, and the dry
moss stuck on the rock
prickles my palm.
I let it drop
for I must find my tongue.
I know it can't be here
in this dry riverbed.
My tongue can only be
where there is water.

પાણી, પાણી,
(pani, pani)

હજુ યાદ છે પેલી છોકરી.
(hujoo yad chay paylee chokri)

"ઠં ડા પાણી, મીઠા પાણી," બોલતી બોલતી આવતી.
('thunda pani, meetha pani, bolti bolti aavti)

માથે કાળું માટલું , હાથમાં પીત્તળનો પ્યાલો.
(mathay kallu matlu, hathma pittulno pyalo)

ઉભેલી ગાડી બાજુ આવતી.
(oobhaylee gaadi baju aavti)

બારી તરફ હાથ લંબાવીને પાણી આપતી.
(bari taraf hath lumbaveenay pani aapti)

અને હું , અતિશય તરસી,
(unay hoo, ateeshay tarsi)

મોટા મોટા ઘૂંટડા લેતી પી જતી.
(mota mota ghuntada layti pee jati)

હજુ યાદ છે પેલી છોકરી.
(hujoo yad chay paylee chokri)
Even water is scarce.
There was a little girl
who carried a black clay pitcher on her head,
who sold water at the train station.
She filled her brass cup with water,
stretched out her arm to me,
reached up to the window, up
to me leaning out the window from the train,
but I can't think of her in English.

II

You ask me what I mean
by saying I have lost my tongue.
I ask you, what would you do
if you had two tongues in your mouth,
and lost the first one, the mother tongue,
and could not really know the other,
the foreign tongue.
You could not use them both together
even if you thought that way.
And if you lived in a place you had to
speak a foreign tongue,
your mother tongue would rot,
rot and die in your mouth
until you had to spit it out.
I thought I spit it out
but overnight while I dream,

મને હતું કે આખ્ખી જીભ આખ્ખી ભાષા,
(munay hutoo kay aakhee jeebh aakhee bhasha)

મેં થૂંકી નાખી છે.
(may thoonky nakhi chay)

પરંતુ રાત્રે સ્વપ્નામાં મારી ભાષા પાછી આવે છે.
(parantoo rattray svupnama mari bhasha pachi aavay chay)

ફુલની જેમ મારી ભાષા મારી જીભ
(foolnee jaim mari bhasha mari jeebh)

મોઢામાં ખીલે છે.
(modhama kheelay chay)

ફળની જેમ મારી ભાષા મારી જીભ
(fulllnee jaim mari bhasha mari jeebh)

મોઢામાં પાકે છે.
(modhama pakay chay)
it grows back, a stump of a shoot
grows longer, grows moist, grows strong veins,
it ties the other tongue in knots,
the bud opens, the bud opens in my mouth,
it pushes the other tongue aside.
Everytime I think I've forgotten,
I think I've lost the mother tongue,
it blossoms out of my mouth.
Days I try to think in English:
I look up,

પેલો કાળો કાગડો
(paylo kallo kagdo)

ઉડતો ઉડતો જાય, હવે ઝાડે પહોચે,
(oodto oodti jai, huhvay jzaday pohchay)

એની ચાંચમાં કાંઈક છે.
(ainee chanchma kaeek chay)
the crow has something in his beak.
When I look up
I think:

આકાશ, સુરજ
(aakash, suraj)
and then: sky, sun.
Don't tell me it's the same, I know
better. To think of the sky
is to think of dark clouds bringing snow,
the first snow is always on Thanksgiving.
But to think:

આકાશ, અસમાન, આભ.
(aakash, usman, aabh)

માથે મોટા કાળા કાગડા ઉડે.
(mathay mota kalla kagda ooday)

કાગડાને માથે સુરજ, રોજે સુરજ.
(kagdanay mathay suraj, rojjay suraj)

એકપણ વાદળ નહિ, એટલે વરસાદ નહિ,
(akepun vadul nahi, atelay, varsad nahi)

એટલે અનાજ નહિ, એટલે રોટલી નહિ,
(atelay anaj nahi, atelay rotli nahi)

દાળ ભાત શાક નહિ, કાંઇ નહિ, કુછ ભી નહિ,
(dal bhat shak nahi, kai nahi, kooch bhi nahi)

માત્ર કાગડા, કાળા કાગડા.
(matra kagda, kalla kagda)
Overhead, large black crows fly.
Over the crows, the sun, always

the sun, not a single cloud
which means no rain, which means no wheat,
no rice, no greens, no bread. Nothing.
Only crows, black crows.
And yet, the humid June air,
the stormiest sky in Connecticut
can never be

આકાશ
(aakash)

ચોમાસામાં જ્યારે વરસાદ આવે
(chomasama jyaray varsad aavay)

આખ્ખી રાત આખ્ખો દિ' વરસાદ પડે, વિજળી જાય.
(aakhee raat aakho dee varsad puday, vijli jai)

જ્યારે મા રસોડામાં ઘીને દીવે રોટલી વણતી
(jyaray ma rasodama gheenay deevay rotli vanti)

શાક હલાવતી
(shak halavti)

રવિં દ્ર સં ગીત ગાતી ગાતી
(Ravindrasangeet gaati gaati)

સૈાને બોલાવતી
(saonay bolavti)
the monsoon sky giving rain
all night, all day, lightning, the electricity goes out,
we light the cotton wicks in butter:
candles in brass.
And my mother in the kitchen,
my mother singing:

મોન મોર મેઘેર શંગે ઉડે ચોલે દિગ્દિગંતેર પાને . . .
(mon mor megher shungay, ooday cholay dikdigontair panay)
I can't hear my mother in English.

III

In the middle of Maryland
you send me a tape-recording
saying "હુવે આ એક વાત તો કહેવી જ પડશે,
(huhvay aa ake vat toh kahveej padshay)

ભલેને બહાર કૂતરા ભસે, ભલે ધોબી આવે,
(bhalaynay bahr kootra bhasay, bhalay dhobi aavay)

ભલે શાકવાળી આવે, મારે આ વાત તો કહેવી જ પડશે.
(bhalay shakvali aavay, maray aa vat toh kahveej padshay)

ભલે ટપાલી આવે, ભલે કાગડા કો કો કરે,
(bhalay tapali aavay, bhalay kagda kaw kaw karay)

ભલે રીકશાનો અવાજ આવે,
(bhalay rickshano avaj aavay)

મારે તને આ વાત તો કહેવી જ પડશે".
(maray tanay aa vat toh kahveej padshay)
You talk to me,
you say my name the way it should be said,
apologising
for the dogs barking outside
for the laundryman knocking on the door,
apologising because
the woman selling eggplants

is crying રીંગણા, રીંગણા door to door
(reengna, reengna)
But do you know
how I miss that old woman, crying રીંગણા, રીંગણા
(reengna, reengna)
It's all right if the pedlar's brass bells ring out,
I miss them too.
You talk louder, the mailman comes, knocking louder,
the crows caw-caw-cawing outside,
the rickshaw's motor put-put-puttering.

You say સુજુ બેન હવે તમારે માટે તબલા વગાડું છું.

(Suju bhen huhvay tamaray matay tabla vagadu choo)

you say: listen to the tablas,
listen:

ધા ધીન ધીન ધા (dha dhin dhin dha)

ધા ધીન ધીન ધા (dha dhin dhin dha)

listen ધા ધીન ધીન ધા (dha dhin dhin dha)

ધીનક ધીનક ધીન ધીન (dhinaka dhinaka dhin dhin)

ધીનક ધીનક ધીન ધીન (dhinaka dhinaka dhin dhin)

ધા ધીન ધીન ધા (dha dhin dhin dha)

ધીનક ધીનક ધીનક ધીનક (dhinaka dhinaka dhinaka dhinaka)

ધા ધીન ધીન ધા (dha dhin dhin dha)

ધીનક ધીનક ધીન ધીન (dhinaka dhinaka dhin dhin)

I listen I listen I listen

ધા ધીન ધીન ધા (dha dhin dhin dha)

I hear you I hear you

ધીનક ધીનક ધીન ધીનક ધીનક ધીન ધીનક ધીનક ધીન

(dhinaka dhinaka dhin dhinaka dhinaka dhin dhinaka dhinaka dhin)

listen listen listen

Today I played your tape
over and over again

ધા ધીન ધીન ધા (dha dhin dhin dha)

ધીનક ધીનક ધા (dhinaka dhinaka dha)

I can't ધા (dha)

I can't ધા (dha)

I can't forget I can't forget

ધા ધીન ધીન ધા (dha dhin dhin dha)

Marie Curie to Her Husband

The equations are luminous now.
They glimmer across my page,
across the walls
across the pillow
where your forehead should be.
You would've smiled at the shape of your graph
which I completed test tube by test tube.

You've managed to slip inside me,
managed to curl your length tightly within my chest.
I want to remind you
of periwinkles, narcissus,
wisteria, iris, laburnum;
the cows that plodded over to sniff,
the handlebars we clutched while bicycling past so many trees,
so many skies and grasses.
Reaching shelter in the dark, each night we'd go
inspect our magic lights, glowing hot
yellow and green, yellow and blue,
caught in rows and rows of bottles.

I now crave grey,
crave rain: days like the one
that killed you keep me
in the laboratory and the lecture halls.
Pierre, this afternoon at one thirty
I continued your lecture at the Sorbonne.
This afternoon
you tossed around in my chest.
Your beard streamed in my veins, my blood. You thrashed,
your legs knocking against my ribs
while I analysed the progress
that has been made in physics.
But at night, I still count in Polish.

Clara Westhoff to Rainer Maria Rilke

No road leads
to this old house we chose.
Its roof of straw scattered
by the loud wind wheezing
its North Sea sounds.
No road leads
to this old house we chose.

I live downstairs
with my clay and stones.
You upstairs
with ink and paper.
What do we do but play with truth,
a doll whose face
I must rework again and again
until it is human.
The clay has gathered all the warmth
from my hands. I am too cold
to touch the marble yet.

Last night the wind blew
my candle out. Tonight again
on the staircase, I
grope my way to your room.
Each night I climb
up these steps
back to you, with your open windows
so close to the wind and stars.
I listen to your poems as I wash
the dust off my skin and hair.
You must have the windows open all night,
I must watch
the straw from the roof
slowly swirl, fall inside
and gently cover your poems.

Tomorrow
come downstairs, will you,
it has been a month.
I want to show you
the new stone I found
stuck in the mud by the dead tree.
Such a smooth globe, not quite white
but honeydew
with a single dark green vein curled across.
Come downstairs, will you, see
the bright red leaves I stole from the woods;
see my lopsided clay
figure bow low down
before my untouched marble.
Tomorrow
come see the ground,
the gawky yellow weeds
at eye level from my window down below.

For Paula Modersohn-Becker

(1876-1907)

The way I returned again and again to your self-portrait with
blue irises
made the guards uneasy.

The way I turned away from your self-portrait with blue
irises
made the guards uneasy.

Was it the blue irises floating around your face, was it
your brown eyes illuminated by something in the blue irises?

How could you know, how could you feel all this
that I know and feel about blue iris?

I was on the top floor with other paintings, other painters,
but unable to concentrate on them because
already I could hear the tone of your voice your brown eyes
would require.

So I rushed back down to be with you.

The look that passed between us was full
of understanding so I could imagine living with you
and arguing with you about whether to put garlic in the soup.

I stared at the blue irises but in my throat
there was the pungent fresh bitterness of watercress.

When I finally left you I noticed three guards following me.

By the time I got home I was furious at them
for witnessing all this.

Eurydice Speaks

Orpheus, I tell you I'm not in hell,
this place is called Maine.
All winter the cold wind burns my face,
and I sweat, wading through all this snow.
But it's spring now:
sounds of snow melting,
water dripping off eaves, flooding crocuses
and jack-in-the-pulpits.
Pussy willows, cattails, forsythia suddenly
awaken junipers tipped with pale new shoots.
The wind flings pine cones my way.
Now walking along the coast
I follow seagulls
with my camera, seagulls
skimming waves and I focus
on their bills in the foaming

water, they dip their bills,
I focus, they rise with limp silver
flashing in the sun as others come swooping
down, I turn circling with my camera
while waves rise and crash upon rocks
flinging salty seaweed and mollusks;
chipping seashells upon cliffs
waves crash and leave small pools of fish stranded . . .
Orpheus, I want to stay here
with the smooth pebbles,
I want to stay here, at the ocean's edge
I have found someone new –
no god, but a quiet man who listens.

3 November 1984

I won't buy
The New York Times today.
I can't. I'm sorry.
But when I walk into the bookstore
I can't help reading the front page
and I stare at the photographs
of dead men and women
I know I've seen alive.

Today I don't want to think
of Hindus cutting open
Sikhs – and Sikhs cutting open
Hindus – and Hindus cutting open

Today I don't want to think
of Amrit and Arun and Gunwant Singh,
nor of Falguni and Kalyan.

I've made up my mind: today I'll write
in peacock-greenish-sea-green ink I'll write
poems about everything else.
I'll think of the five Americans
who made it
to Annapurna without Sherpa help.
I won't think of haemorrhageing trains
I'll get my homework done.

Now instead of completing this poem
I'm drawing imlee fronds
all over this page
and thinking of Amrit when we were six
beneath the imlee tree
his long hair just washed
just as long as my hair just washed.
Our mothers sent us outside in the sun
                    to play, to dry our hair.
Now instead of completing this poem
I'm thinking of Amrit.

The Undertow

There are at least three
languages between us.
And the common space, the common dream-sound
is far out at sea.
There's a certain spot, dark
far out where the waves sleep
there's a certain spot
we always focus on,
and the three languages are there
swimming like seals fat with fish and sun
they smile, the three languages
understand each other so well.

We stand watching, jealous
of the three languages, wishing
we could swim so easily.
But the waves keep us back,
the undertow threatens;
so we take one word at a time.
Take 'dog' for example,

કૂતરો (kootro) in Gujarati, *Köter* in Low German
Hund in High German, like hound in English.

Dog   કૂતરો   (kootro)   *Köter*   *Hund*

hound   *dog*   *Köter*   કૂતરો   (kootro)

કૂતરો   કૂતરો   કૂતરો
(kootro   kootro   kootro)

The waves come chasing
the dogs on the beach
the waves come flooding the streets
listen to the seals swimming
through the bookstores, listen
the words spill together,
the common sounds
ક ખ ગ

શ ક્ષ સ

kö   kh   ga

sh   ksh   ß   spill together

spill together
filling our shoes,
filling our love with salt.

At the Marketplace

Look at the young jade-coloured artichokes!
Shall we have some for dinner?
Yes? No?
But wait. Look, there's fish in the next stall –
Oh to eat raw fish and raw onions and fresh
lemon juice and more raw fish –
juicy salt.
Eating raw fish
it doesn't matter if it's raining –
cold, and the umbrella
is blown aside – Eating raw fish
makes you feel like a mermaid through your legs –
Juicy salt.
I always crave sea salt, sour salt, strong eel salt.

Now there are purple sea horses all over her
and she is becoming a mermaid with artichoke skin.
Purple sea horses that he branded last night –
on her neck, shoulders, thighs: acrobatic purple,
elegant tattoo tails plunging deep into eel salt.
Sea horses are sucking on her salt
and she is talking like a mermaid, reasoning like a mermaid;
sea horses growing fuller and dark fat purple
and she eats another raw herring, swallowing
like a mermaid.

The Writer

The best story, of course,
is the one you can't write,
                    you won't write.
It's something that can only live
                    in your heart,
not on paper.

Paper is dry, flat.
Where is the soil
for the roots, and how do I lift out
entire trees, a whole forest
from the earth of the spirit
and transplant it on paper
without disturbing the birds?

And what about the mountain
on which this forest grows?
The waterfalls
          making rivers,
rivers with throngs of trees
elbowing each other aside
to have a look
at the fish.

Beneath the fish
            there are clouds.
Here, the sky ripples,
the river thunders.
How would things move on paper?

Now watch   the way
                    the tigers' walking
        shreds the paper.

Go to Ahmedabad

Go walk the streets of Baroda,
go to Ahmedabad,
go breathe the dust
until you choke and get sick
with a fever no doctor's heard of.
Don't ask me
for I will tell you nothing
about hunger and suffering.

As a girl I learned
never to turn anyone away
from our door. Ma told me
give fresh water, good food,
nothing you wouldn't eat.
Hunger is when your mother
tells you years later
in America the doctor says
she is malnourished,
her bones are weak
because there was never enough
food for the children,
hers and the women who came
to our door with theirs.
The children must always be fed.
Hunger is when your mother is sick
in America because she wanted you
to eat well. Hunger is
when you walk
down the streets of Ahmedabad
and instead of handing out
coins to everyone
you give them tomatoes, cucumbers,
and go home with your mouth
tasting of burnt eucalyptus leaves
because you've lost
your appetite.
And yet, I say nothing
about hunger, nothing.

I have friends everywhere.
This time we met after ten years.
Someone died.
Someone got married.
Someone just had a baby.
And I hold the baby
because he's crying,
because there's a strange rash
all over his chest.
And my friend says
do you have a child? Why not?

When will you get married?
And the bus arrives
crowded with people hanging
out the doors and windows.
And her baby cries
in my arms, cries
so an old man wakes up and yells
at me: How could I let
my child get so sick?
Luckily, just then
someone tells a good joke.

I have friends everywhere.
This time we met after ten years.
And suffering is
when I walk around Ahmedabad
for this is the place
I always loved
this is the place
I always hated
for this is the place
I can never be at home in
this is the place
I will always be at home in.
Suffering is
when I am in Ahmedabad
after ten years
and I learn for the first time
I will never choose
to live here. Suffering is
living in America
and not being able
to write a damn thing
about it. Suffering is
not for me to tell you about.

Go walk the streets of Baroda,
go to Ahmedabad
and step around the cow-dung
but don't forget
to look at the sky.

It's special in January,
you'll never see kites like these again.
Go meet the people if you can
and if you want to know
about hunger, about suffering,
go live it for yourself.
When there's an epidemic,
when the doctor says
your brother may die soon,
your father may die soon –
don't ask me how it feels.
It does not feel good.
That's why we make
tea with tulsi leaves,
that's why there's always someone
who knows a good story.

Brunizem

for Michael

Brunizem, I say
and brummagem.
I have the jack of hearts
in my pocket – yes
he was waiting for me
on a shelf
in a thrift shop.
But he is more than the jack of hearts
and he kissed me.
I still keep the card
in my pocket.
Brummagem, I say
and brunizem.

The other night
I dreamt English
was my middle name.
And I cried, telling my mother
'I don't want English
to be my middle name.
Can't you change it to something else?'
'Go read the dictionary.' She said.

I've been meaning
not to mean anything for once.
I just want to say, 'brunizem!'
I feel brunizem
when this man kisses me
I want to learn another language.

Well, Well, Well,

How can I tell you about it
without using those words again?
I need words like *witch, power,*
maybe even *gypsy* – I don't know.
But I need *witch*. Will you grant me that?

Blood-salty egg yolks soft boiled 3 minutes,
the colour of Africa on my wall map.

These mornings it takes 5 minutes
to figure out where I am.

Sometimes bone-marrow is pure.
Pure and innocent and clean.
Sometimes bone-marrow is delicious.
Delicious and pure and innocent.
They taught the 4 year old girl
to suck out the young goat's fresh marrow.
After that she refused
to sleep alone.

When night spiders crawl on brown gypsy skin
they leave silver trails behind.
You try to brush it away
thinking it's bits of spider silk.
But it's deeper. You can't wipe it off.
Your skin will soak it up, your blood will keep it.

Arno Peters has rediscovered the world.
On his map
Africa is a large ochre-ripe papaya.
America lurks
in detergent green shadows.
I know I've made the mistake
of loving America too much.

Afterwards she wanted to eat tomatoes and raw onions.
Then numbers made too much noise
around her forehead,
and if she closed her eyes she could see the insides
of books she'd read.

Chew on pine-needles and look at the moon.
Then you'll know what to do.
If you taste the difference between
topology and topography it'll make the difference.

When I say *witch* I can't have you thinking of Medea
or Macbeth or Salem.
I can't have you thinking at all.
After she swallowed the bone marrow
she could control
the blood in her brain.
If she wanted a silent nothing
she could make it in her brain.

What is magic? What is freedom?
His favourite leather jacket, gentle grey,
that he gave her, has power. When she smells it
she finds the words she needs. Slowly the jacket
is beginning to smell of her,
so when he wears it again

he'll smell of her and he'll know exactly
what to do, exactly where to go.

Sometimes if you get lost in America you'll see freedom:
Silver threads hanging from trees,
wet silver around that horse's mouth.

He told her to put the 'h' back
in *Osterthorsteinweg*. So she did.
She does so everyday: Magic *Osterthorsteinweg*
on clean envelopes.

If the tomato is *rot*
then I'll always imagine rotten tomatoes.
Although *rot* isn't pronounced like rot.
Although *rot* can be red as red bursting ripe fat red
as spurting red as ready to be cut up and cooked
immediately red. That's *rot*.

When he discovered she was a witch it was easier.
Then she could feel at home with him.
And as for him, well, he was looking
for a witch who would speak to him.
She was surprised.

When she brings Iowa April maple leaves indoors
her brain refuses to sleep,
her bone marriw makes different blood.
Then all night she hears *Osterthorsteinweg* and Hölderlin.
All night she understands the parts of Hölderlin
that I don't understand.

I've fallen through the cracks of vocabulary lists.
Below all grammar rules. And then what?
Can there be anything without grammar?
Well, there are tomatoes growing everywhere.
My fingers smell of their leaves.

When the witch spoke to him, when she touched his hands
he got some magic,
he got what he was looking for.

Although she had no intention
of giving him any. It just happened.
For a while she was cautious, uncertain.
Then she let him
have all the magic he needed.

Where is the common ground?
Arno Peters decided to trim Europe down
into pink bits.

I'm trying to figure out how the waters stay apart.

What does it mean to feel at home?
Sometimes when you walk into a house
and wander through the rooms until you feel the doors
and windows snug around you,
when you walk across the wooden floors and feel
blood clots in your throat then you know
it's the wrong house.

What if it's the wrong country?

He knew how to make pictures with her magic.
And so it was good.
When she had to leave *Osterthorsteinweg*
her magic wanted to turn into a lioness.
When she had to leave her magic became
distraught and out of focus so he gave her
his leather jacket.
The next day when she woke up she was
in the wrong bed, she was in the wrong country.
It took her 5 minutes to figure it out
with reason and logic. But there's no
freedom in logic. No logic to freedom.
No magic in logic.

How can she feel at home in so many places?
How do gypsies know when to leave?

If you brew tea in the strong teapot
with the good force in your fingers

and the long thoughts in your head during
the silver season then . . .

They taught the 4-year-old girl to pick tea leaves.
They needed tender young fingers to break off
the most delicate leaves. They taught
the 4-year-old girl to massage the legs
of 80-year-old men and tired
pregnant women. They needed tender young
fingers to ease out the burning muscles.
Afterwards they fed her the young goat's
fresh marrow.

Once while backpacking up the Appalachian trail
somewhere in Massachusetts I met freedom.
She was tall, 5′ 10″ and had long white hair.
She said she was almost 60.
It was the end of August.
She'd been on the trail since Georgia
and was headed for Maine. She was alone.
I thought she was a dream. But I can show you
how she moved,
how she bent her head when she combed her hair.

That's why Arno Peters had to change the map.
That's why I took the word *witch.*

There are magic coins in the leather jacket.
Something burns whenever she touches them.
If she buys anything with those coins she'll lose
the power. She wears a turquoise blouse to cool her blood.
She wears silk to cool her magic, her logic . . .

from

MONKEY SHADOWS

The Langur Coloured Night

It was a cry
          to awaken the moon.

A sound to make the moon shout back.

It was the truth
            from a young langur.

It was a cry
          shining with moonlight,
a cry resounding against
white stone verandahs.

It was the langur
mirrored in that moon in the pond –
and the moon's face doubled
in the eyes of the langur.

It was the langur poised
                    grim-faced
                    stiff-haired
          between leaps.

It was a cry to breathe life
into the moon, the stones . . .

It was the langur
          just frozen, silver-jewelled with the moon.

It was the langur
              on his way to a tree.

It was a cry
          meant for no one
          but the moon – dear friend
of the langur who reveals the hiding places
of dogs, cats and even snakes.

It was the langur
              doing whatever he wanted to do

now that everyone is asleep.

The Stare

There is that moment
when the young human child
stares
at the young monkey child
who stares back –

Innocence facing
innocence in a space
where the young monkey child
is not in captivity.

There is purity
  clarity
there is a transparence
  in this stare
which lasts a long time . . .

eyes of water
          eyes of sky
the soul can still fall through
because the monkey
has yet to learn fear –
and the human
has yet to learn fear
          let alone arrogance.

Witnessing it all
one can count eyelashes
one can count the snails
in the grass
          while waiting
for eyes to blink
waiting to see who
will look away first.

Still the monkey looks
at the human not in the same way
he would look at leaves
or at his own siblings.

And the human looks
at the monkey knowing
this is some totally other being.

And yet, there is such good will
such curiosity brightening
their faces.

I would like to slip inside
that stare, to know
what the human child thinks
what the monkey child thinks
at that very moment.

Remember, the human child
is at that age
when he begins to use words
with power
but without the distance
of alphabets, of abstractions.

Mention bread
and he wants
a slice, buttered and with honey –
immediately.

Mention the cat
and he runs over
to awaken her.

The word
is the thing itself.

Language is simply
a necessary music
suddenly connected
to the child's own heartbeat.

While the young monkey child
grows at a different rate,
looks at a tree, a bush,

at the human child
            and thinks . . .
Who knows what?

What remains burning
is that moment
of staring:
the two newly formed heads
balanced on fragile necks
tilting towards each other,
the monkey face
        and the human face
absorbing each other
with intense gentleness. . . .

Nanabhai Bhatt in Prison

At the foot of Takhteshwar hill
there is an L-shaped house
hidden from the road
by five mango trees
planted by Nanabhai Bhatt.

Huge crows swoop over
the L-shaped terrace,
red-beaked green parrots fight over
the mango trees. Some years the monsoons
sweep away too much.
It is 1930, 1936 . . .
It is 1942:
Nanabhai sits writing for a moment
while my grandmother
gives orders to everyone.

The next day, he lands in prison again:
thrown in without a trial
for helping Gandhiji,
for Civil Disobedience.

One semester in college
I spent hours picturing him:
a thin man with large hands,
my grandfather in the middle
of the night, in the middle of writing,
between ideas he pauses to read
from Tennyson, his favourite –

A hand that can be clasped no more –
Behold me, for I cannot sleep,
And like a guilty thing I creep
At earliest morning to the door.

What did he make of the Northern trees?
The 'old yew', the chestnut . . .
and the strange season of falling leaves
that comes every year –
Did he spend hours trying
to picture it all?

I know that
as a student in Bombay
he saved and saved
and lived on one meal a day for six months
just so he could watch
the visiting English Company
perform Shakespeare . . .

And I spent hours
picturing his years in prison:
Winter 1943;
it is dark in his cell.
He is sixty years old.
I see him
sitting cross-legged on the floor
and I wonder what he knew
by heart, I wonder
which lines gave him the most comfort.

That semester was endless
with a restless Baltimore March

when the tight buds on the forsythia
teased our blood.
And I, impatient to get on
with other writers
had to slow down
to study that same poem.

So much information
swallowed like vitamins
for finals –

and yet, I paused at every turn
wondering which parts he had loved.

What Happened to the Elephant?

What happened to the elephant,
the one whose head Shiva stole
to bring his son Ganesh
back to life?

This is the child's curiosity
the nosy imagination that continues
probing, looking for a way
to believe the fantasy
a way to prolong the story.

If Ganesh could still be Ganesh
with an elephant's head,
then couldn't the body
of that elephant
find another life
with a horse's head – for example?

And if we found
a horse's head to revive
the elephant's body –
Who is the true elephant?
And what shall we do
about the horse's body?

Still, the child refuses
to accept Shiva's carelessness
and searches for a solution
without death

*

But now when I gaze
at the framed postcard
of Ganesh on my wall,
I also picture a rotting carcass
of a beheaded elephant
            lying crumpled up
on its side, covered with bird shit
vulture shit –

Oh that elephant
            whose head survived
for Ganesh –

He died, of course, but the others
in his herd, the hundreds
in his family must have found him.
They stared at him for hours
with their slow swaying sadness . . .
How they turned and turned
in a circle, with their trunks
facing outwards and then inwards
towards the headless one.

That is a dance
            a group dance
no one talks about.

Understanding The Ramayana

When they bowed
to us in their sparkling robes
I didn't want them to leave –

that day felt scorched
from the beginning;
unbearably hot
as if it were perpetually noon.

No cool imlee scented
                    Poona breeze,
so we had retreated
into the shadows cast
                    by our house.

We were tired, almost bored
when we saw them unfasten the latch
to the gate like thieves and slip through
into our garden before
anyone could stop them.

We were only children then
still we admired the fitted
yet comfortable sleeves
partly covering their furry arms –
arms which were a slightly different
                    brown from ours.

And I envied the tailor
who had stitched such earnest
headdresses – a tailor who
I thought was privileged to be
designing clothes for such creatures.

Sita, I stare at
          the longest.
She was so refined,
the way she folded up
her hands for *namaste*, while the slant

of her neck told us everything
about a disciplined suffering.
And the swift darting of her eyes
between Rama and Lakshman
required no words.

So it didn't matter
that none of them could speak.
We could even have done without
the whiny drone of the narrator
who also directed them, waving
his hands about with such force
as if that would sharpen
Sita's emotions.

It didn't matter
that now and then we glimpsed
a looped up tail
motionless as if drugged to sleep
beneath their costumes.

Their tails were fanned by swishing hems
when they leaped –
Sita flying away in fear;
Rama flying in for a fight
          to save her.

Bright pink and orange frills
speckled with blue-green sequins
and outlined with silver
threads, zig-zagging stars –
bright frills would flutter up
revealing the quiet tail – its power
dormant and forbidden to take any part
in the actions of Prince Rama
                    or Princess Sita.

We felt relieved to know
the narrator hadn't chopped off
or even shortened
the glorious question marks
curling behind their backs.

Only Hanuman
allowed to use his tail
was the most joyous
and felt perfectly cast.

Monkeys more humane
than anyone –
But it relieved me to see
a flash of pride, of anger
cut through their meek faces.
Or was it only acting?

Where had they been found?
And how had they learnt
the meaning of *The Ramayana*
that well?

So absorbed were we
as if we had never heard
this saga before,
that we didn't mind
the withered, small-pox
scarred face
of the man who owned them;
we didn't pay much attention
to the chains around the delicate
monkey feet – preventing them
from jumping very far.

In the end our only regret
was that we couldn't join them
when they were dragged away
by their worn out master.

We stood in the middle
of the garden
watching them leave –
our hands hanging limp
by our sides.

They seemed to disappear
into haloes of swirling dust.

The gate clanged shut
          and the heat
descended like a curtain
forcing us back
          into the shade.

Angels' Wings

I can recall that age
very well: fourteen-years-old,
when I thought I understood
Lenin and Mao,
and Christina Rossetti was beginning
to sound silly.

One April Saturday morning
after swimming lessons
I stood waiting for my father,
pacing the formaldehyde
                    stung corridor,
I twirled equidistant between
the autopsy room and his office.

My eleven-year-old brother
                              and I together
but silent for a quarter of an hour
as if all that swimming, all that chlorine
had altered our breathing
had washed away our speech.

A heavy door opened and a man,
dark as the shadows he cast,
a man with electric white hair
asked us to step inside.
There was something
he wanted us to see.

The room was festooned with wings,
all of a similar shape
            and strangely human.
Perhaps fairies' wings
            or angels' wings, I thought,
made of real gossamer . . .

As we stepped closer
we could see clumps of clogged cells,
those grape-like clusters meant to blossom with oxygen
now shrivelled
beside rivers of blood choked black.

They were not drawings,
not photographs –
but human lungs
well-preserved by someone's
skill in histology.
He could tell us how old
their owners had lived to be
for how many years each had smoked.
He would tell us everything
except their names.

Twenty pairs of lungs
pinned up on his wall:
a collage of black and grey,
here and there some chalky yellow
                        some fungus-furred green.

How long did we stand there?
And what did we say?
I don't remember eating lunch
or what we did
for the rest of that day –
Only those tweny pairs of nameless lungs,
the intimate gossamer
of twenty people I never knew
lungless in their graves.

Mozartstrasse 18

for Eleanor Wilner, who first asked me
to describe post-war Bremen

I am sitting in the *Spielplatz*
around the corner from Mozartstrasse
wondering
where guilt ends
and where it begins;
while the children dig in the sandbox
and the sixteen-month-old boy
I'm looking after, pours sand
onto my lap.
I don't see how guilt
could possibly begin here.

And yet,
there are buildings in Bremen
I can't help considering evil.

And there is this dream
that does not leave me –
beginning gently one night
with me going downstairs, out
of the house,
my hand on the rain-dripping gate –
that's when I see them:
They are all there,
an international crowd
all dressed exquisitely in black and white,
full flowing black coats
a glimpse of white linen collars . . .
Their presence makes the damp morning
warmer, the air
takes on the smell of fresh coffee
and chocolate from their clothes.

They walk slowly, just like tourists
with plenty of time.
They come up the adjoining street
towards Mozartstrasse, towards me

while I stand by the gate.
Not a word is spoken
but they all greet me and point
to this house, number 18.
They greet me with their eyes
full of questions, there is something
they want to ask me, but I cannot guess
what it is. Not a word is spoken
but they all stare deep into my eyes,
separately
each with his own questions,
each with her own questions.

I remember all their eyes, all dark,
dark, but each with a different darkness,
a field of dark flowers
and tree trunks completely covered
with hundreds of dark butterflies . . .
that's when I first try
to speak, to move,
to say at least 'hello'.
But I can't.

I continue staring into their calm eyes
fresh and clear
as if they all had had a good night's sleep.
And I think, how strange, as I stand
fixed by the gate,
they seem to know me, how strange
that they don't speak and why are they pointing
at this house?

Mozartstrasse 18. Is it important?
Does it matter where we live,
what happened before?
I wonder
while the children dig in the sandbox
and the sixteen-month-old boy
I'm looking after, pours sand
onto my lap.

It is one thing to know
what happened before
but quite another to read the list
of names, of streets, of houses . . .
It is one thing to know
what happened before
but quite another to live here today
and to find out precisely who lived where
in 1937, 1938 . . . To look through
the original *Bremer Adressbuch*, complete with advertisements,
and then to follow up with 1983 statistics.
Who was arrested, shot.
Who got sent to Minsk, who escaped . . .

For example, the Ries family
who lived at Mozartstrasse 25,
Albert and Emma with their two children,
Günther and Cäcilie, left for the United States
on the thirteenth of December 1938.
Their house is no longer here.

But number 18 remains a mystery.
Theodor Gruja, *Damenschneider*
lived here, with his shop upstairs.
There are five other tenants
in this building, listed in 1937.
This building of 1854, where
I feel so free with these four metre high ceilings,
tall windows everywhere to let in the light.
The perfect place for a tailor,
I tell the landlady as we sit on the balcony
trying to guess what happened to Theodor Gruja.
Over coffee and cake she tells me
about the thousands of needles
she found all over the floors, pins and needles;
about his Jewish wife
sent away to America. *Thousands of needles*
she repeats, and pins even stuck in the walls.
That was 1975, she says, when she bought
and restored the building, saving it from demolition.
Thousands of needles, and no toilets, she says

pointing to the spot in the garden
where the outhouses had been.

Why so many pins even stuck
in the walls?
I see rivers of needles streaming silver
paths from one room into another –
Who threw everything
onto the floor? Who took the sewing machines?
Who took the clothes? I see rivers full
of needles, flickering wet gills,
and in a shifting
trick of sunlight they could be
just hatched salmon I watch from a cliff top,
smelt lashing silver trails.

It is April now
and the huge sprawling chestnut tree
has small leaves,
small as a six-month-old baby's hands.
We talk about the tailor's Jewish wife
and I look at the tree
with an impatient tightness in my legs,
knowing it was here for all those years –
as if I could blame it, let alone
question it . . .
Now there are these lengthening days:
April, May, June, the chestnut leaves grow larger,
and our rooms are filled with so much light,
so I can't stop thinking
about Theodor Gruja, *Damenschneider*,
and his wife.

Wine from Bordeaux

Today I've invented a man
who has bought two thousand bottles
of a 1985 wine from Bordeaux,
the *Bois-Malot* which won
the Bronze Medal in 1986.
And now this 1985 *Bois-Malot* has become
even better than gold, and it will stay
good, it will delight you
          for years to come.

Over here, in Ostertor
you and I would have to pay
about *vierzehn Mark* for a bottle.
But I'm sure my imaginary man
has worked out some special deal
with the shopkeepers, maybe even
with the people
          who planted the grapes.

He's bought two thousand bottles already
and plans to buy more.

1985 is the year
before Chernobyl.

He doesn't like
to ingest anything harvested
                    in Europe after 1985.

'This wine goes very well
with New Zealand lamb,'
he confides to the wine shop owner.
'It's the only meat
I feel safe eating . . .' he whispers.

No doubt
he's got a large cellar
to hoard all those bottles
of crimson Bordeaux

with their handsome brown labels.
I imagine him smiling
at their sharp dark winks –
          rows and rows of rounded shadows
each time he opens the door.

There's another man
I can tell you about.
He is real.
He got himself sterilized
in May 1986 when he was eighteen
because he was convinced
his chromosomes were damaged.
And he didn't want to pass on
          any mistakes.

While the women
who gave birth over here
in 1986 sometimes didn't know
          what to eat.

I imagine some of them still
scrutinize their children
with fear, wishing they could supervise
the health of every cell.

While in the towns near Chernobyl
embryos didn't make it
fetuses didn't make it
and the babies who managed
to get born and who managed to grow
into children – suddenly
become sick with leukemia.

But the child
that I still think of
was one eight-year-old boy
who loved playing in the sand
          like most children
who didn't notice dirt or mud on his clothes
          like most children –

But then he started begging
to be allowed to take a shower
whenever he came indoors
thinking the water
        thinking the water would wash
                it all off –

A Story for Pearse

But the more fragrant body,
the body that was love, rose up,
no rot as yet set in,
evicted the people from the wake,
and raced out the door
after the soul that had been so faithful,
and fell, by the lake's edge, without
seeing the soul again.

None of the mourners was there
to bury either body.

– Pearse Hutchinson, 'The Soul that Kissed the Body'

Reading your new book today
I am reminded of my great-aunt,
of her soul, her body . . .
How she died alone
with a terrible stench
oozing from her body –
how almost no one mourned her.

Oh the lucky Soul
that felt moved to kiss life,
to kiss the Body before departing!

But your version, your lines
seem also written for her –
and all day your words with their urgent movement
have been pulling my mind
back to my great-aunt.

My great-aunt Hirabhen
was rescued from her mother-in-law
rescued from her husband
soon after she was married.

Her mother-in-law used to beat her
with a bamboo pole.
She made her work all day
with little food,
then whipped her every night
until her pretty skin turned ugly.

At least they didn't pour kerosene over her head,
at least they didn't set her ablaze.

But who knows what finally compelled
the young woman Hirabhen to tell her parents
          in those days
to go to a court of law
where the judge said:
'This is no marriage! You are free!
You can choose again,
you can decide for yourself – '

She chose to become a nurse
to earn her own money.
She said she wanted
                    to learn something new
to help others.

But I am certain
that her soul walked out
on her that day in court.
After the battle was won
there was nothing more

for the soul to say –
after she was free
she could never feel her soul again.

The soul was gone
                    to the lake
in a forest where no one
                    could follow.

She had a life full
of naked bodies – diseased
patients broken with bedsores
and married doctors who enjoyed
                    lying with her
enjoyed tricking her
into believing anything.

Then, for a long time
there was always a different man
invariably weird and coarse
compared to her delicate face.

What was it she searched for in the body?
In the blood cells, the plasma, the hair,
the eyes, the eye-lids –
In the length of a scar . . .
Was it the way to recognize death
                    from far away?
The way death flings its own light
                              around a body
unmistakeably marking it?
The medicine? The dosage? The numbers?
Numbers defining fevers,
chemicals, hours, years . . .

What was it she wanted to learn?

The time it takes
                for stitches to heal?
The time it takes
                for a scar to fade?

But I am certain
she could never feel her soul,
                her self.

It was easy for everyone to say
she should have found God
like her older sister
who was happily married and blessed
                with children.

It was easy for everyone
to say *what* she should have done.
And, no doubt, they thought
she had done something
to deserve her fate.

I wonder if she ever
spoke to God.
I imagine she would have given up
with a Lord who allows torture.
And how would she have continued
believing in a God who dwells
in every heart? The Lord
in her mother-in-law's heart?
The Lord in her husband's heart?

Towards the end
when she was truly old
and I had just stopped
          being a child – and I had just been told
about her life –
I was afraid of her paranoia
afraid of her frantic-caged-animal-fear,
her disjointed spat out speech
          I couldn't follow.

What did flowers mean to her?
And colours?
And birdsong?
How bird shadows screech
chopping up the tropical light –
Did she care?

What did children mean to her?
Sometimes I think my mother,
her patient niece, was the only
person, the only child
who ever consoled her.

Towards the end
when she was dying
(and my mother was not informed)
she used to gaze at herself
naked in the mirror
arching her neck, head tilted
in a way that once was coy.
Did she see
her cracked smelly skin?

Did she have a more fragrant body,
a second body that was love?

Towards the end
when she was dying
she used to poke her naked chest
with a tired finger
as if to say *here* *here*
this is where
my soul used to be.

Groningen: Saturday Market on a Very Sunny Day

The large eye was still fresh,
perfectly intact: the size of a cow's eye
and the iris, black.
Clean black against the white eyeball.
Oh who will buy this fish-head
with a cow's eye?
The eye remained stuck while looking up
at the nets, at the surface of the water,

at the shadows cast by the bottom of the boat . . .
or after being yanked in
it looked up at the sky, the knife,
at the blank face of the busy fisherman –
it looked up
with the lethargic sadness of cows
and the Renaissance emotions of praying peasants.

One by one, at different times,
the six of us separate in the crowds,
distracted at every corner
by something new – one by one
this afternoon at different times
somehow we all saw
this particularly thick fish-head
with a sad cow's eye.
And in the evening, simultaneously
we all started to speak of it.
'Oh who will buy, who would dare buy
that fish-head?' we wondered during supper –
unable to say more.
We were strangely thirsty.
Thirsty, thirsty,
that night
we couldn't drink enough.

Counting Sheep White Blood Cells

for Jo Shapcott

It was like being ordered
                    to count the stars
and to classify them
by their size, their brightness –

And it was like being ordered
to count all the tiny wild flowers
in a never-ending field
          and to name them –

There were days
when she, the lab technician
would sit staring through the microscope
for five hours straight
counting sheep white blood cells.

It didn't put her to sleep.
Instead, it made her eyes feel powerful,
it made her feel wired
as if she were the source
of electricity for that microscope.

Whenever she looked up
to put in a new slide
the lab whirled
          unreal around her
for she had gone with all her dreams
into the galaxies of sheep.

It was the macrophage she wanted,
the one cell that doesn't grow
in vitro – her missing secret
to understanding
the immune system.
But she had to count
and yet discount the lymphocytes
and leukocytes and the large
erythrocytes getting in the way.

And they were beautiful
strangely rounded flowers, these corpuscles,
some fuzzy dandelions
          gone to seed
but still intact, translucent
balls of cotton –
Some prickly burrs
          stuck fast together
so she can't forget
the sheep, the tangled wool
full of rain and grass . . .
Some fuzzy dandelions

gone to seed – but there was
no time to admire them.

Across the street
          in the hospital where
she also worked, people tried to live
with cancer.

She was eighteen
and always kept her notebook handy.
A notebook full of numbers, drawings . . .
entire pages crossed out
          leading nowhere.
At the end of the day
she would feel so numb.

That was a time of living
in a different vocabulary:
laboratory Latin.
But also: *we've sacrificed the animals.*
    We've harvested the cells.

That is how
she started to speak.

The Fish Hat

1

For weeks this is how
she has been dreaming of herself.

So far, she can manage
to imagine shadows
draped over her scooped out parts.

Her dream shadows mimic the shape
her flesh used to take
before the surgery.

But the shadows are blue
as if she were a Hindu god,
                    a divine hermaphrodite –

Yellow edged with red
clings to her neck and wrists.
It's the sort of yellow one sees on signs
warning of radioactivity –

And there are holes
you can see right through;
holes, where her nipples used to be.

Her hands are young
are knotted together into a tight ball
                              hanging pear-shaped . . .

Her face looks like a cutting board
as if some intern had practiced on it.

There's a fish hat she designed
herself long ago when she was twelve:
Homage to a baked fish, ready to eat
complete with fork and knife
and a thick slice of lemon.
A fish hat that has turned
as blue as her own shadows;
a fish hat that now seems glued
to her head through all these dreams
after the surgery.

2

It almost looked like something
that had come out of the sea.

But I had never seen
 an opaque jellyfish
with a single, round, closed eye-lid.

They brought it over in a rush
first thing in the morning
the nurse running with the styrofoam box
padded with ice. 'This is not my job!'
I wanted to say.
'You are supposed to dig out the tumours
yourself. What happened to the surgeon?'
I wondered. But I didn't speak.
I was afraid my voice would break –
afraid my voice would affect my hands . . .

I had to make an incision into the centre
and watch the sphere collapse.

The movement must feel like pulling out the calyx
 of a large flower
of a fully blossomed rose
one doesn't want to destroy –
then watching the petals scatter –

except that I had to consider the blood,
I had to try
to cut out a segment
of a tumour without blood. I had to spend
the rest of the day analysing that tumour.

3

After Picasso painted her
 he laughed.
It was a big joke.
He showed her off
to all his friends . . . At least
this is what you think.
As we stand in the museum
you picture them *once upon a time*

drinking litres of red wine, toasting her
surrounding her hollow blue shadows
and laughing, laughing
especially at the fish hat.

The Echoes in Poona

One day the pure, clean rhesus monkeys
gagged on the sun,
on their half-eaten ripe fruits,
and now their screams for Hanuman
echo through the jungle
as they spit out the moon, the stars . . .
If you look closely
you can see where
the nets have left marks
across their thin fingers.

They shake their heads
trying to dislodge
the grinding noise of jeep tires
on dirt roads.
Their tails still expect
to brush against leaves, grass . . .
and their neck muscles
are not used to this sudden
lack of wind.

From our garden,
when I stand near the bougainvillaea
I can hear their caged cries
echoing, echoing – freshly torn
from the heart of the jungle.
They shy away from the wires,
at first they even flinch

from each other.
They are wild with rage
echoing, echoing –

After a few days
they are quiet, a young mother
turns to stroke her sister,
a louse is found, removed. Soon
their fingers work to search each other –
They take their time, such gentle care,
as they reinvent their family.

Such pure, clean rhesus monkeys,
uncontaminated specimens:
Forced helpers in the search
for vaccinations and antibiotics.

Meanwhile the men who watched the hunt
from their small tents
are now busy focusing microscopes.
My father also
spends his days counting
monkey kidney cells in vitro.
He scrubs his hands
until they bleed, until the skin
starts peeling. He bathes
several times a day
while colleagues less careful
die from the disease.

From our garden
I can see the back of the building:
rows of air conditioners
drone against the noise
of the new rhesus monkeys.
One day my six-year-old brother begins
a new game
where he visits the monkeys
and feeds them flowers, lost in his game
he gives them branches with berries
while the tired watchman,
skinny Satnarayan, almost dozes –

And my tired father, lost in thought
in his windowless room
examines test tubes,
his eyes straining against
the fluorescent lights.

Years pass.
Microscopes improve.
My father will soon retire.
These days, when my year-old daughter
wants something
from the kitchen table,
from the shelves, her arms thrusting out
like a trapeze artist,
her urgent *hu hu hu* speech
reminds me of those monkeys – and last week
when she cried hot with fever
and tense with antibiotics
I lay sleepless through 5:00 a.m.
remembering the bold black eyes
of the caged baby monkeys
eager with surprise as they pulled
on sap-wet weeds with berries
offered by my brother –
their dark velvet fingers grasping for
the bruised yellow and bruised red
velvet fruit.

Walking Across the Brooklyn Bridge, July 1990

In New York
children are being shot
to death this summer.
It's usually an accident.
Someone else, no doubt an adult,
was meant to be killed instead.
It's not a war,
just a way to settle disagreements.

Walking across the Brooklyn Bridge
one feels removed from everything
as if one were passing by
          in a low flying plane.
Below, on both sides the cars
stream by. Above, the steel
cables converge, tighten.
The muscles in my legs feel
exposed, worn out.

The children somehow get in
the way: They're found dead
in the car, in the house,
in the crib. Sometimes it happens
that the father
was cleaning the gun.

Walking across the Brooklyn Bridge
today I see work being done.
Repairs. Clean, clear-cut
adjustments. Renovation.
The humming of steel against wind
drills through my bones –
it's driven up my spine.
The humming does not end.

But the worst case
I read about didn't involve a gun.
Simply a father, newly arrived from Montana
who decided to feed
his six-day-old son
to a hungry German Shepherd.
Was the mother really asleep?

Walking across the Brooklyn Bridge
I pause, look around.
What is real in this symbol,
in that other one over there . . . ?
The steel cables have become a cage,
a sanctuary. Whose cage?
Whose hope?

In another section
of the newspaper I read
about the ever growing problems of refugees.
Who will take them in?
Especially the ones from Vietnam,
a favourite subject for photographers:
flimsy boats, someone's thin arm in the way –
Who can forget those eyes?
And who can judge those eyes
that vision?

Walking across the Brooklyn Bridge
even on a hot afternoon
one sees many joggers.
And there is the view, of course.

Looking across the water
I think of those people from Vietnam.
The mothers, the fathers,
what they wouldn't have given,
what they would still give –
their blood, their hair, their livers, their kidneys,
their lungs, their fingers, their thumbs –
to get their children
past the Statue of Liberty.

Rooms by the Sea

for Michael

It's summer all right.
This light makes me think
of June in Miami
July in Ocean City
August in Cape Cod.

This heat reminds me of a certain freedom
this light is the colour of a certain freedom
we had one summer –
the freedom to want
a child, the longing to let life go on
as it pleases.

The heat has flung the door wide open –
and the light is constant.
The cry of our imaginary child
breaks our afternoon nap,
untangles our sticky thighs . . .
The sea is a loud salty glitter
pounding against the shore, back and forth
back and forth, as if driven by nervous fishes.
The light remains steady
and the heat is constant –

Someone, we don't see,
has stepped inside
and walks through the kitchen, that we don't see.
I imagine you
grabbing a beer
from the fridge.

The sofa burns red
the carpet crackles green
and the picture in the pine wood frame
is fading away.

Franz Marc's Blaue Fohlen

I want to meet
Franz Marc's blue foals.
I see them in a secluded field
in a place like Kentucky or Dublin.
They make the morning glories miserable
as they run through the blue grass of Kentucky,
they make the morning glories miserable
as they run through the endless wet
June blue-gold light of Dublin.
I want to find their blue ears
and unravel some riddles.
I want to nose their blue necks.

Love in a Bathtub

Years later we'll remember the bathtub,
the position
          of the taps
the water, slippery
as if a bucketful
          of eels had joined us . . .
we'll be old, our children grown up
but we'll remember the water
                    sloshing out
the useless soap,
the mountain of wet towels.
'Remember the bathtub in Belfast?'
we'll prod each other –

29 April 1989

She's three-months-old now,
asleep at last for the afternoon.
I've got some time to myself again
but I don't know what to do.
Outside everything is greyish green and soggy
with endless Bremen-Spring drizzle.
I make a large pot of Assam tea
and search through the books
in my room, shift through my papers.
I'm not looking for anything, really,
just touching my favourite books.
I don't even know what I'm thinking,
but there's a rich round fullness
in the air
like living inside Beethoven's piano
on a day when he was
particularly energetic.

The Need to Recall the Journey

for Regina Munzel

Now when she cries
        for milk,

now as she drinks
        I drift back
to the moments when she was
almost out

still part of me
but already I could reach down
        and touch her hair.

I want to return
to her moment of birth.
It was too quick.
I want it to go on –

When the pain was suddenly
defined by her head,
when she was about to slide out
          safely
all by herself – I felt my heart
go half-way out with her . . .
like seeing a beloved one off
to a harbour, to a ship
destined to go
to a far away place
          you've never been to . . .

But I could touch
          her hair –
a thick, fuzzy heat.
Sticky feathers clung
wet to runny whites of eggs . . .

But this is a little person
who already has
a favourite sleeping position.

Weeks pass, the bleeding stops.
Months pass –
What I thought could never heal
actually heals.

And still there is this need
to recall the journey,
retell the story.
The urge
to reopen every detail
until our faces glow again.

What are we
trying to understand?

How we walked for hours
while *she* kneaded herself
out of my womb;
how we paced up and down
the small room – circling
the huge bed.

No one can explain these details.
No one could have prepared
me for this.

The sound of ripping
silk, tearing skin
comes from within me.

Machines are recording everything
one might like to know.

Afterwards, I thought:
how lucky to have been alert
as any animal
struggling to give birth

in a cave

or behind a grove of trees

or in an open field

now walking, now straining to push,
now lying down
without drugs – no anaesthesia.
How lucky to have felt
each step. The sharp
scalping blackness
as if one had swallowed
thorns, entire cacti
and splinters from a knife . . .

Fallen fruits burst
into slippery juice.

Fat roots that once pulled
sucking up salt:
sobbing voices from the sea –
fat roots let go
    snap away
then break apart like rubber pipes
full of blood.

Is this how it feels
to be almost drowned?

    Black, black,
    that old knowledge
    from the earth.

And I stopped
listening to T-Bone Walker
and then Telemann, I was told
spinning out loud from the cassette.

How everything irritated
me except your hands
    your voice.

No one can explain
    these details.

A thousand rivers collided
    rushing
and changed direction
within my chest.

And then, she was out
she was taken away
to be washed, bathed –
She was taken to be examined.

And then, I was cold.
Cold, as if my bones
had been emptied
    of their marrow.

Until Our Bones Prevent Us from Going Further

for Michael

We spent all day
            in a jeep –
our hands awkward
with questions, our speech twisted
with confusion as the jeep strained
winding higher and higher through the mountain,
                        at eye-level with flying eagles –
we stared back at a vulture who possessed
                                    the only tree for miles . . .

Now the sky begins to feel
like a ceiling we can just barely touch,
maybe
by springing up and then uncoiling
stretching out with a snap
                until our bones
prevent us from going further.

The sky is taut wet silk:
          someone's blue wings,
                      panting through a sweaty gleam –
          someone's blue kite
                    longing to melt.

It is the sort of blue that makes us
think we can find
answers to all our questions.
Where shall we live? What shall we do?
Shall we ever
          have a child?

I brought you *here* to unwrap my fears,
to pull out words only the Himalayas
could translate
and rephrase with their ringing echoes.
But now
it is the blue that hisses back
                          silencing us.

Now the red tongue of the sun
licks us until we forget our patterns
our different plots
we thought so important.

We have just arrived
at a *gompa*. But we hide
behind the stones by the entrance, not wanting
to interrupt the flow
of *om mani padme hum*
                that ripples through the rows
of boys reciting lessons
                with old monks.

Oxygen-weak air
rushes through our lungs
making our blood dizzy – we shudder
as if someone, some spirit
          who lives in such thin air
were reshaping our brains, our dreams.

We watch as if we too were praying
as if they were praying for us.
There are only stones where we stand.
But something stirs, I feel
            a sliding movement –
What *is* that? Rocks skitter.
My soul skuttling away.

We watch, not daring to move.
Those fresh-blood-maroon robes
ruffled by the wind are the only lotuses,
the only flowers between
the dusty stones and the blue-lidded sun.
The eight-year-old boys
just losing their milk teeth
chant as if they had learnt this rhythm
from some ancient insects
with enormous wings, no longer possible today.
Now they pause, now they follow
the old monks, descending slowly

into a new chant. We are allowed
to enter.

And now it is your turn
to weep, the gold
blue-shadowed dust stings your face
as you turn with the wind, towards
the light, towards the broad chest
of the mountain – you weep
alone, you stand tall
your head thrown back, you weep
and I am still far away
down at the bottom
looking up, just starting to climb the steps
while you weep because
it is more than beauty, more than truth,
more than suffering, more than the firm gentleness
of this infinite treeless blue that glows
over these maroon robed children –
you weep and weep
and I suddenly know
never again
will I need to justify
my soul to you.

from

THE STINKING ROSE

The One Who Goes Away

> *There are always, in each of us,*
> *these two: the one who stays,*
> *the one who goes away –*
> Eleanor Wilner

But I am the one
who always goes away.

The first time was the most –
was the most
        silent.
I did not speak,
did not answer
those who stood waving
with the soft noise
of saris flapping in the wind.

To help the journey
coconuts were flung
from Juhu beach
into the Arabian Sea –
But I saw beggars jump in
after those coconuts – a good catch
for dinner. And in the end
who gets the true luck
from those sacrificed coconuts?

I am the one
who always goes away.

Sometimes I'm asked if
I were searching for a place
that can keep my soul
from wandering
a place where I can stay
without wanting to leave.

Who knows.

Maybe the joy lies
in always being able to leave –

But I never left home.
I carried it away
with me – here in my darkness
in myself. If I go back, retrace my steps
I will not find
that first home anywhere outside
in that mother-land place.

We weren't allowed
            to take much
but I managed to hide
my home behind my heart.

Look at the deserted beach
now it's dusk – no sun
to turn the waves gold,
no moon to catch
the waves in silver mesh –

Look
at the in-between darkness
when the sea is unmasked
she's no beauty queen.
Now the wind stops
beating around the bush –

While the earth calls
and the hearth calls
come back, come back –

I am the one
who always goes away.

Because I must –

with my home intact
            but always changing
so the windows don't match

the doors anymore – the colours
clash in the garden –
And the ocean lives in the bedroom.

I am the one
who always goes
away with my home
which can only stay inside
in my blood – my home which does not fit
          with any geography.

We are Adrift

At night
our sunroom is closer
to the water –
we are adrift with the moon.
Fog clings to the glass panes:
sticky cobwebs torn apart
          remain floating –
Where are the spiders?

Something swirls
          and swirls
pulling us closer
          to the Juan de Fuca Strait.
The foghorn blows
louder each time
making us think
of hoarse sheep
and frogs by marshy fields.
The foghorn sounds closer
each time, warning us
of Trial Island – we can't see
the blue-bottle-greenish light
flashing anymore, never mind
the four skinny poles lit up
with red lights.

We imagine everything
through the bud-taut branches –
our sunroom is adrift
          in the fog.

We've heard about those who never
returned from these waters
we've heard about those who
were rescued. We should be quiet.
Maybe the dead
have different rules
over here.
Maybe there are others
adrift in these currents.

Although She's a Small Woman

Although
she's a small woman
she can make
the fog leave Quatsino Sound.

Watch her now
without her clothes
she stands at the front
of the canoe – the waves
become lullabyes
as she sweeps her arms
to the north, to the south –
Her wrists are so alert
her song so sharp
the fog decides to lift
itself up and go
somewhere else.

And southward on the shore
there's the turtle-crow-man
the tall cedar man

waiting for this fog –
he likes to swallow
while cloudy strips.

Ages later a Japanese girl
will poke that faded
turtle, fearing splinters
from the cedar, she'll be
surprised to feel skin
like soap, like fog,
as if a bolt of silk hardened
into wood
she can run her hands down.

'Man Swept out to Sea as Huge Wave Hits Rock'

– *Times-Colonist*, Victoria, BC, 7 January 1992

Freak waves, rollers,
tsunami . . . tsunami . . .
Harbour waves.
Tidal waves out of the blue
they say it happens
from time to time.

Soon the wave felt heavy,
entangled with legs and arms
that were too slow –
and the fish felt a man
flailing against sea weed –

It's reported the rock he stood on
was 15 metres high,
that he was 56 years old,
and he stood 13 metres away
from the shoreline.
But can they make a graph,

a sketch, can they find
the proper equation? Can they tell us
what to do
so it won't happen again?

Was the sky too blue
that day in Ucluelet? How cold
was the water? Why did the wave pounce,
why take him away so he was never
found? Why must such a perfect
meditation be rent, rent body and soul
through and through
so you and I shiver, pull each other
nearer to the shore when we
walk by the same place.

How Far East is it Still East?

One Japanese fishing boat lost at sea
was found with a skeleton
curled up inside.

What happened to the others?

Nights when it was windy
the whales could hear the rattling bones.

How could so many Japanese
fishing boats get lost?

There were rules in 1639, rules
about the size of the boat,
rules about how much food
they could carry –

Food enough to make a man
turn back home,
hungry.

How far east is it still east?
And how far west is it still west?

Somewhere in the North Pacific
the waters part

the waters part
only because we think they do –
but how could the ocean
really be split in two?

Where are your stars?
And where is your sky?

Which way do the waters part
for you? Which way will you let
the currents take you?

Now what is this voice that says:
'Go away. This is not
your world. You can't enter
this water – it's too dark for you.'

Only the whales listen
to the skulls trapped
in the Japanese fishing boats.

Now what is this voice that says:
'Go away. This is not your world.
Only the whales can answer
the lost fishermen.'

How far east is it still east?
And how far west is it still west?

Which way will you let the currents take you?

Of course, the women saw them first.
The women on their way
to collect wood –
the women on their way
to begin something –

At night they will whisper
to their elders:

Today two men walked out
of the sea – we watched them
eating berries – we do not know

if they are really human.
Today we saw fifteen whales
not far from the place
there the men walked out
of the sea –

Polish-German Woodcarver Visits Vancouver Island

for Hannes and Jutta

Arbutus, ash, cedar
Douglas fir –
and most of all, driftwood.
He takes whatever strikes
his shoes, his fancy –
whatever lies unwanted on the ground.

A walk is not a walk
without his knife flinging slivers
of wood, left right and centre
along the way.

The blade peels, scours,
gouges uphill and down –
the blade wants
to hide away in wood.

His hands balance
the trees and the sky
differently from you and me.

Whether a piece of wood
will give a fish
or a man with a sharp face
is something only the knife knows.

Meanwhile the road
keeps winding. His young sons
dart back and forth.
Meanwhile his wife watches
starlings with beaks full
of parsley, build a nest.

Whether the wooden man
will carry a duck
in his arms, or a baby seal
with a strange tail
is something
only the knife knows.

Maybe the time of year matters.
For example,
it is April now.
Maybe the thin moon
meddles with more advice.

His hands
understand stories
hidden to us.
When he goes
to meet a totem pole
you can be sure
the knife burns.

Salt Spring Island

for Phyllis Webb

You wore purple
and Salt Spring Island flashed
green through your windows.

The way you spoke the words you spoke
reminded me of Gandhiji.

And then it was time
to catch the ferry back to Swartz Bay.

Even today I find Gandhiji's words green like yours
green like Salt Spring Island –
Those words live with your eyes
flashing and your purple blouse gentle
gentle in my mind, your colours
your words – and now I've put a paintbrush
in your left hand.

Your Sorrow

You take your sorrow with you when you leave.
However wide the sea or sky between,
the journey's end will bring you no reprieve.
– Peter Sacks

But what if you change
and your sorrow becomes
your memory, a broken bone,
a finger that heals strangely
forever crooked for the world to see
so even your thoughts don't match up –
and yet there's no pain left.

Isn't there a place
that would make you forget?
A sky that would make you

disagree with yourself – ?
A sea that would toss
your sorrow back in your face
shattered into a hundred,
a thousand different questions?

I don't know.
Is it reprieve
the journey's end should bring?
Or is it enough
simply to have gone away –
to have gone away so far
for so long that finally reprieve
is too gentle a word, too one-sided
for what you need,
for what you've already stepped toward.

The Light Teased Me

for Georgia O'Keeffe

The light teased me
          all day –
the light made me
          doubt every word.
What do I mean? What
          have I gleaned
                    so far?

By late afternoon
when I stumbled across
your *Red Poppy*
I couldn't see
          the *Poppy* anymore.

Instead, a fat tarantula emerged
rich with eggs, I could tell
by the way she moved.

A black sheen of joy.

Then she slid back into scarlet
            scraps of silk.

Cow's Skull – Red, White and Blue

There's something very right about it.

It's truthful, direct,
to the point – but also awkward,
ugly, brutal.

Imperfectly perfect.

Red blood.
White bones.
Blue sky.

When all the young men in America
could only think of Europe,

she walked through New Mexico
collecting bones.

Red blood.
White sky.
Blue bones.

Those days she gathered horses' skulls
and cows' skulls instead of flowers.

I see her staring at the skulls,
looking through the eye-holes –
            for hours.

Red sky, blue sky,
red blood
white bones, white sky –

She understood the land.
And when she left that place of dry heat
she took a barrel full of bones
back to New York.

Skinnydipping in History

for John Ashbery

First, you think of water and then, of course, the surface of the
water.

Arms reaching out for air, for light, breaking the glassed-in-
water-picture of trees.

It's best to begin in the middle of the story: to plunge right in

to the heart of things, to the sort of place where dolphins can be
found – if you know what I mean

There was the young man born in Japan but not Japanese
who spent his youth in Chile, who spoke of skinnydipping day
after day
with his sixteen-year-old schoolmates, studying the light on
naked limbs
while his mother planned dinner parties for Allende. Things
happened so quickly
as they always do. Afterwards, when they searched Allende's
body
they found that boy's father's phone number. You bet they
dialled that number endlessly
to find out why. That boy, who's not such a young man anymore
once recalled Chile in a long sentence beginning with skinny-
dipping one afternoon
and ending with Allende's death and the telephone no one
wanted to answer.

So much action in one sentence, so much noise.

One has to return to the surface for air.

There is so much we know, too much, cruelly, to be expressed in any medium,
Including silence. And to harbor it means having it eventually leach under

Your deepest thoughts will come to nothing if they don't surface.

There's something to be said for waiting for that most wanted

that most desired thing (whatever it is) to surface.

If you start thinking of the surface as *a visible core,*

not superficial but a visible core, it'll make you forget the knife.

After all, why would you need to cut through the core? What do you think you'd find?

Don't we all know how even what you eat changes the surface of your skin.

It's true. You are what you eat. **Der Mensch ist, was er ißt.**

All of a sudden one realizes that *a yak is a prehistoric cabbage.*

If you have ever seen the glaring yaks in Ladakh eyeing the vegetables,

while the prehistoric smell of cabbage being cooked engulfs you as you walk by

the houses in Leh, then you'll understand the importance of the surface.

In fact, *the one thing that can save America*

is a slant version, a new mythology, a revision of its surface.

So what if *the juice is elsewhere.*

One day the juice might seep through and jazz up the surface.

One day a man will make a gesture you have never seen before.

One day a man will touch a piano in a way you never thought possible.

And how will the houses in Connecticut look then?

Will there still be people with big backyards

and green lawns to mow all summer?

Nothing is Black, Really Nothing

1

nada es negro, realmente nada.
So Frida Kahlo wrote
one day in her diary.

But Frida, how black you could paint
your pulled-back hair, your braids,
and the little dark hairs above your lips –
How black your eyes
your eyebrows;
how black the hairs of your monkey
especially in *Fulang-Chang and I.*

But nothing is black.
True black that breathes
must shine with blue light,
green shadows – some say
a reddish glow means
the colour isn't black enough.

2

Then there was *elephantinum,*
elephant-tusk-black.
For Plinius records the tale
of Appelles, born
around 350 BC, he was
Alexander the Great's blue-blooded court painter –
he was the first
to create the colour called *elephantinum*
from fired ivory.

Dry distilled from tusks,
the fat fired out
from the elephant tusks . . .
and in the end black powder extracted,
distilled,
dry, dry . . .

And you can extract black
out of grape seeds.

And you can extract black
out of wood or gas
or out of that oil hidden deep within
the earth.

How black do you want
your paint?

3

I do not want
to consult the dictionary
for words about black,
I know those one-sided words
already: a black heart, a black mood,
a black day, a blunt black-jack –

I keep brooding instead
over my daughter's love for black –

How when she was not quite three
and the blond children teased her
for having brown hair,
she was only angered
by their inaccuracy.
'This is not brown!' she screamed
holding up a fistful of her hair.
'It's black!
My hair is black, black –
Not brown!'

As if to say
she knew her colours well.
She no longer confused orange with red,
indigo with violet,
or brown with black.
She could understand light green, dark green,
yellow, blue, she learned
          the names so quickly.

4

Now I keep turning back to you, Frida –
Nothing is black
but how you loved your black hair
that's not really black
and how many different black strokes
you found (when nothing is black)
to pull out every shade
          of blackness
from your hair, your self –

The Blue Snake Who Loves Water

for Michael

Outside
it's an Indian-summer-black
Iowa night.

Inside
I sleep alone
and I dream an afternoon picnic
in a tropical garden.

Outside
it's a harmless, flat
corn-fielded, dry night.

Inside
where I sleep alone
the grass is wet
and the blue snake
who loves water
has entered my dream.

'Watch out! A snake!'
everyone yells –
And it's strange
that I am not afraid.

The snake is on his way
to the lake. In no hurry
and yet, with no time to waste
he slides towards us –
everyone runs away
but I see no reason to move
or even to sit up
for he can easily slip
over me, which he does
sliding across my right shoulder
and pressing against my neck
as he leaves.

Outside
it's morning, already hot
this Iowa-bright prairie air.

Inside
I'm wide-awake – the tea steeps
and my neck burns
at the very spot the snake
touched as he slid
over me.

Outside
I meet my love
by the Iowa River.
We talk about dreams
about snakes – we have just met
a few weeks ago.

Still, I try to explain
the blueness of the snake
the burning on my neck –
How can a dream
be more than a dream?

No one will ever
believe me.

No one, except maybe the river.

Last week the river was a muddy slur.

But now full of blue sky
the river bends and smiles
and becomes a 'she'.
The river narrows
her metallic glinting eyes
sun struck – the river smiles
as if she could believe
in my blue snake.

The river smiles
as if she felt the blue snake
rushing through her.

It Has Come to This

The Chiefs:
Rain in the Face
Red Cloud
Long Dog
Charging Hawk
Young Man Afraid of His Horses
Crow Foot
Kicking Bear

In a museum, in a German city
I greet your photographs.
Your names give me a story
I can't write,
a story I can only dream
on warm nights.

Burial of the Dead
at the Battle of Wounded Knee S.D.
CopyRighted Jan. 1st 1891
by the North Western Photo Comp.
Chadron Neb. No. 1.

Who owns the dead? Who owns
the burial? What would you say
Sun in the Pupil
Red Shirt Girl
Has a Dog
Spotted Thunder
Cast Away and Run
Wounded in Winter
Shedding Bear
Shake the Bird
Bring Earth to Her?

Your names are stuck
in my mind – I want to keep
them: I want to imagine the eyes, teeth,
voices, fingers – that lived in your names.

The Stinking Rose

Everything I want to say is
in that name
for these cloves of garlic – they shine
like pearls still warm from a woman's neck.

My fingernail nudges and nicks
the smell open, a round smell
            that spirals up. Are you hungry?
Does it burn through your ears?

Did you know some cloves were planted
near the coral-coloured roses
to provoke the petals
into giving stronger perfume . . .

Everything is in that name
            for garlic:
Roses and smells
            and the art of naming . . .

What's in a name? that which we call a rose,
By any other name would smell as sweet . . .

But that which we call garlic
smells sweeter, more
vulnerable, even delicate
if we call it *The Stinking Rose.*

The roses on the table, the garlic in the salad
and the salt teases our ritual
tasting to last longer.
You who dined with us tonight,
this garlic will sing to your heart
to your slippery muscles – will keep
your nipples and your legs from sleeping.

Fragrant blood full of garlic –
yes, they noted it reeked under the microscope.

His fingers tired after peeling and crushing
the stinking rose, the sticky cloves –
Still, in the middle of the night his fingernail
nudges and nicks her very own smell
        her prism open –

Ninniku

1

Ninniku, ninniku
the Japanese said
as they examined the Buddhist
monks. *To bear insults*
with patience on the way to Nirvana.

The Buddhist mind
is strengthened by the sharp
light of garlic.

White . . . White . . . is the flame of garlic
        the heat of garlic.

Then Queen Maya, Siddhartha's mother
dreamt that a white elephant
entered her womb.

White –

And that was the colour of the swan
Siddhartha rushed to save.

White –

And that was the colour
of Kanthak, the horse he once rode.

White –

And that was the colour
of the elephant he once rode.

The Japanese met Buddhism
and *ninniku* sprouted
along with the lotus.

om mani padme hum
the monks whispered
ever sleepless, ever vigilant,
every day they walked for miles –

for the body must be able
to bear the Truth,
for without the body the mind can not
climb the steep path of right mindfulness.

om mani padme hum
the monks whispered
with garlic on their breath.

2

Ninniku:
To bear insults with patience.
That's what they have to do,
those immigrants
from the garlic-eating regions.
Some travel north
and some travel west
but they all learn to keep their distance.

Sometimes the women
            in desperation
douse themselves with perfume –
musky jasmine
            husky rose –
later on the bus, humid
vapours mingle with garlic
on their skin and clothes; only sharpen
the luminous
homesickness
in the whites of their eyes.

Garlic in War and Peace

In peace they rubbed garlic paste
across their lower backs
before they lay together.
A slow cleansing – it was
sticky, then strangely cool.
It was their secret bite
their strongest aphrodisiac.
And they preferred green garlic
with large purple cloves.

In war they dabbed garlic paste
over each wound –
such endless wincing
and endless those white cotton bandages.
The stench of pus and garlic
finally giving way to pink skin
shiny as a freshly peeled clove
of garlic – new patches of skin
reminding them how in peace
their garden overflowed with lilies
and garlic – and the roses!
The roses sprayed with garlic-water.

In peace their only war
was against the worms.

Frightened Bees

Notes from a Welsh Herbal

Take a clove of garlic
prick in three or four places in the middle
dip in honey and insert in the ear
covering it with some black wool.

And if I had no black wool
would white wool do –

or must it be at least red
or dark blue?

Let the patient sleep
on the other side every night
leaving the clove in the ear
for seven or eight nights unchanged.
It will prevent the running of the nose
and restore the hearing.

Black wool I found at last
but it makes mc dream
of frightened bees with a dead queen –
          homeless
swarms rushing in a panic –

night after night – the dead queens
are piling up fast – but someone wants
to crush them with rose petals
and honey – someone wants to eat
the dead queens and taste
a sweetness
          a knowledge no one dares to try.

A Brahmin Wants the Cows to Eat Lots of Garlic

So he can drink
the garlic-rich milk.

That's the only way
he's allowed to take garlic.

For three days and three nights
he'll wait, let the garlic seep into
the cows, he'll wait for the right moment.

A brahmin wants the cows
to eat lots of garlic –
so he watches and he sings *bhajans*
making sure they do.

He wants to step out
of his brahminhood and wander
cow-like through the spring-hazy-purple dust,
cow-dust.

But a little bit of milk
will bring him back to his senses.

If You Named Your Daughter Garlic Instead of Lily or Rose

She would travel far
to gather mushrooms –

After a night of rain
she would rescue snails,
putting them back on the broad leaves,
the high stems able to support them.

She would never lose
a crop of tomatoes.

You would never know
she was Garlic
because she would smell of roses –
her garden overflowing with fennel –
She would travel far
to gather mushrooms, that daughter
you named Garlic.

And unlike Tolstoy's Varenka
she'll meet a man
who won't mind
talking about mushrooms.

The Pharaoh Speaks

I feel heavy, sticky. I've been
too tightly bound and squeezed shut.

Still, how good it is to be alone
at last in my tomb –
Amidst all the gold and lapis lazuli
they've hidden six bulbs of garlic.

My soul has come back
for one last visit. My soul hovers
by the garlic and prays.

The gold laughs
and sings of its golden self –
daring my skin to achieve
          such a perfect colour.
The lapis lazuli tries to put a blue
          spell over me.

But the six bulbs of garlic remain self-contained –
quietly odourless,
saving their power for something else.

It Has Not Rained for Months

> *To know whether a woman will bear a child.*
> *Clean a clove of garlic, cut off the top, place it*
> *in the vagina and see if next day her mouth smells*
> *of it. If she smells, she will conceive; if not, she will not.*
>
> – Hippocrates

It has not rained for months.
Hot dirt from the fields, hot dust
whipped up with the wind
hurts my throat, my chest –

I can not breathe
and then he comes with his clove
of garlic, with his hot garlicky breath
and his beard, sharper than thorns
and his face of stone – I can not breathe
but he opens my mouth

and then I must keep this clove
of garlic inside where my flesh
has become so raw
that it burns – It has not rained
for months – and I lie facing the window
and I watch the crows
peck at stolen seeds –
I can not breathe
and every morning he comes
full of remorse with his hot
garlicky breath he opens my mouth

and then I must remove
this clove of garlic
from this burning flesh
                    and I think that if
I would bleed at least
the blood would heal
me, at least the blood
would soothe
                    the garlic scrubbed cuts.

It has not rained for months.
I am wet from my own sweat.
Hot dirt from the fields
stuck in my heart.

Every month I bleed
too much –

too much – and then he comes
with his clove of garlic
and then I must keep
this clove of garlic deep inside me
where it burns.

An India of the Soul

It is not necessary to have poems full of mendicants and minarets, gurus and ghats, to contemplate an India of the soul.

– Alastair Niven

But the soul will be the colour of turmeric
spilt on white stone.

And the creature who lives in the soul
will count with her thumb
on the joints of her fingers.

Time will be slow
and Time will be concrete
and Time will be stuck
like a wet crow peering down
from a tree, broken and black –

Who is more jagged, the tree or the crow?
The crow peering down, his head so crooked
so tilted –

Then the soul will be the colour of ferns
surrounded by mosquitoes.

And the creature who lives in the soul
will wash her feet
before going to bed.

A Gujarati Patient Speaks

A heart surgeon in London made it a practice to operate only after he and his patient had both listened to Gould recordings.

Usually, when I'm sick
I eat rice with yoghurt,
two cloves of raw garlic
and some દાળનું પાણી (dalnu pani).

After the dal has settled
on the bottom of the pot
I scoop out the top-water,
rich in onions and garlic –
I squeeze fresh lemon juice
over it in my bowl,
drink it slowly –
Usually, I feel much better.

Coriander is important.
And fenugreek.
I use lots of fenugreek.

Although I live in London
I still prefer my ways.
Sitar, tabla: I call them my basic
instruments because they help me
improve my mood, soothe my headaches.

When I hear certain notes
I can smell patchouli,
I can smell my mother's soap
and the oil she used
          on her hair.

So when my doctor asked me
to listen to all this Bach,
the *Goldberg Variations* –
I thought he must know
something about Ayurvedic methods.

But why Bach?
And why Glenn Gould?
Normally, I don't listen
          to piano.
Even my children prefer saxophone –
          and mostly jazz.

Still, this morning after breakfast
I gave it a try.
Glenn Gould: such movement, exact

the way honeybees measure
            and remeasure the sun
all summer – pink zinnias –
urgent wings hum after
the shifting angle of earth and sun.

And if there is sleep in the background
it is the sleep of a man
with too many dreams –
and it is the sleep of lovers
who can't ignore each other.

I can see why a surgeon
would worship the gestures,
lust after the fingers behind this sound.

But me? How will the piano
understand my moods?

Genealogy

My daughter
when she was four
once described herself as a tiny egg,
so small, she was inside me
at a time when I was still not born
when I was still within her grandmother.
And so, she concluded triumphantly,
I was also inside Aaji.

When she showed me
her newest painting, she said:

At night the sun is black
and the moon turns yellow.
Look, that's how I painted it.
This is the sky at night
so the sun is also black.

What are the angels doing at night?
It's not bad to die
because then you can become
an angel – and you can fly and that's so nice –
I'll be happy to be an angel.

Later, I overheard her say to her father:

When I am a grandmother
I'll be very old
and you'll be dead.
But I hope you've learned
to fly by that time

because then you can
fly over to my house
and watch me with my grandchildren.

Fate

i.m. A.K. Ramanujan (1929-1993)

Of course, you would smile
if you knew that I've decided
to insert fate
telepathy and unconscious 'second sight'
at the core of this poem.

Let fate be an elephant who needs water,
walking along the x-axis
and let telepathy be a young scorpion:
fast, hungry, scurrying down
the y-axis – we do not know,
perhaps we'll never know if they meet.
Only the monkey called *second sight* knows
and he won't tell us unless
we pass a certain test, unravel
a certain trick.

But how shall I explain
that day I dropped everything
that needed to be done,
turned instead to your books
started re-reading them
one after the other in a great rush
stayed up most of the night
alert, nostalgic,
I hunted out my favourite lines
not knowing that all the time
you lay in hospital.
Not knowing why
I had this sudden craving
for your words.

You were still in Chicago,
I in Bremen, and the Ganga still flows
dirty and oblivious.

Forgive me if I call it fate
or some form of telepathy.
But very soon the phone rang
at an odd hour with the news
of your death –
while your books were still strewn
around me so full of book-marks,

they bulged
some like paper flowers
some like paper birds
trying to open petals, wings –
little fans of magic
            with their own dreams
refusing to fit back
into the tight slots on the shelf.

Orpheus Confesses to Eurydice

1

It was a lack of faith.
I admit it. I didn't believe enough
in you or even in the power
of my song. I needed constant reassurance.
Yes, I saw how the Furies wept
as I sang slower, softer – Time stopped for me –
still, I didn't think they'd let you go.
I didn't think you'd be free to follow me.
And so I looked back
wondering: *were you really there?*

I've caught the snake
that killed you – I keep him
alive. He's become a sort of pet –
such a small viper, and so supple –
my last connection to you. And his brightness:
eyes, skin – how he shimmers in the sun – keeps me alert
and reminds me at times of your brightness:
the sun in your hair, the jewels around your neck.

At first, of course, I thought of revenge.
I thought of hurting the snake,
              of throwing him into a fire.
But I hesitated and now I've grown fond of him.

2

Once when I stood singing by the cliffs
a sharp stone fell – and then a lizard
darted to the east and her sliced-off tail
rushed away to the west – and I watched
the tail shudder and jerk –
a yellow-green thing in such a hurry.

Now I've become a torn-off
lizard's tail. Only my tongue lives
in my bodiless head – my tongue still sings
against the noise of the river.

Maybe this is what I really wanted:
To be just a tongue –
a lizard's tail without the lizard.

To be a pure voice
without my tired, awkward body –

Now I'm almost weightless and about to be swallowed
by the ocean – I will become
a stronger voice.

Jealousy

I go to bed and then that man
sits in the next room and continues
laughing about his own writing.
And then I knock on the door
and I say, 'now Jim,
stop writing or stop laughing!'
– Nora Joyce

A woman eats her heart out
and the window near her bed is too small
and it won't shut
properly – and her heart tastes
quite sweet, very nice despite the bitterness –
but the moon doesn't care
and anyways the moon stopped
helping her long ago.

The opera is just over
and a crowd of footsteps,
so many high heels, clatter
past her window

There are no stars tonight.
Only clouds that move
too quickly and make her dizzy.

She'll close her eyes
but she won't sleep
she'll continue to eat her heart
                              out all night –

And in the morning she'll think of a way
to fix the window.

More Fears about the Moon

1

Fetus after fetus lost.

And the inner voice
dares not speak to me.

Each time I looked
there was always too much blood.
I could never see the face.
Only the fins: limp,
but they glistened and once,
the curved spine seemed to tremble
in the dish.
Too many little ones slipped away
from me. My girls,
my boys – couldn't wait
to leave – my crooked fishes
my sea horses – they didn't want
to become children.

Fetus after fetus lost.
Can't you take me away
from this city?

2

The full moon kept us
awake all night.

And in the morning
her ghost smile took us
out to the ocean,
made us walk for hours
along the edge of sand and water.

Soon we came to the place where the dolphin lay.

The dolphin lay far inland,
dead – thrown up by some great wave.

We circle it. The split open bruises,
bloated purple – the torn skin.
You cover its eyes with mussel shells.
And we walk on – but return
the next day and the next, everyday
until the tide shifts.

3

Now each day the ocean comes closer.

It crawls, it leaps, this rising tide –
while the moon shrinks.

We watch from the doorway.

What if the waves never turned back,
but kept on rising, higher and higher?
What if the moon lost control
and let the tides go as they please?

Sharda

After all these years
my mother has forgotten her name –
the name of the girl
she most admired –
the girl who lived across the street
when my mother was little.

So I tell her
it must have been Sharda.
Sharda:
A mature name, full of dignity.
Sharda, who is the lute: Veena –
light sun-notes flicker
transparent across blood-dark
heavy tones – Sharda who is both
Sarasvati and Durga –
dragonfly wings
shimmer, curious above the drowned squirrel –
How can one name
contain so much?

'Sharda, Sharda!' I can see
her mother calling her.

Sharda was a serious girl.
She wore a silk *chanya choli:*
that is, a long full skirt and a tight
bodice-blouse – she sparkled.
She was nine-years-old.
She knew many prayers.
She sat alone
in the *puja* room –
she was doing *arti*
she was ringing the small brass
prayer bell with one hand
and holding a small flame
also brass cupped in her other
hand – when she slipped
and the *ghee* spilled across

her silk clothes and the wick
spit fire over her fingertips.

Maybe there was a gust of wind –
something fluky
so even the huge crows fled
with their elbow-wings.

Why was there nobody
at home that day?
Why was there no one
who heard her cry?

'Such things happen,'
My mother says.
I suspect Sharda's elders.
Did she have too many sisters?
'No, no! It wasn't like that.'
My mother shakes her head.

Still, we can agree about how
she spun, hopping around
and around
trying to escape the flames.

Then she was sucked in –
it was like a sudden wave
a wall
with a sharp undertow –
A fire-wave
almost silent
compared to water.

'Sharda, Sharda!'
My mother must have called
for a long time
even after they found her.

Frauenjournal

A woman kills
her newborn granddaughter
because she has four already.

A woman kills because
there's not enough money
not enough milk.

A woman kills her newborn daughter
and still eats dinner
and still wears a green sari.

Is this being judgemental?
Or is this how one bears witness
with words?

And another woman in another country
makes sure that her seven-year-old daughter
has her clitoris sliced off
with a razor blade.
This is what they will show us
tonight – prime time –
We're advised not to let our children watch this.
This has never been filmed before.
Sometimes it's necessary
to see the truth. The moderator tells us
words are not enough.

Now the camera focuses on
the razor blade – so there is no doubt
about the instrument. The razor blade
is not a rumour.

Now the camera shifts over
to the seven-year-old face:
she smiles – innocent – she doesn't know.
The girl smiles – she feels important.
And then the blood and then the screams.

Why do I think I have to watch this?
Is this being a voyeur?
Or is this how one begins
to bear witness?

And another woman tells us how years ago
she accidentally killed her own daughter
while trying to cut out her clitoris.
The risks are great, she tells us,
but she's proud of her profession.

How much reality can you bear?

And if you are a true poet
why can't you cure
          anything with your words?

The camera focused
long and steady on the razor blade.
At least it wasn't rusty.

How can you bear witness
with words, how can you heal
          anything with words?

The camerawoman could not
afford to tremble or flinch.
She had to keep a steady hand.
And the hand holding the razor blade
did not hesitate.

And if you are a true poet
will you also find a voice
for the woman who can smile
after killing her daughter?

What is the point of bearing witness?

Afterwards, the girl can barely walk.

For days the girl will hobble – unable

unable unable

unable to return
to her old self,
her old childish way of life.

Consciousness

I am so red now
and I sparkle –
So the fuchsia sulks – jealous.

And a woman walking by
dreams a silk blouse
in my colour would suit her.

I am so red now
the children have been warned
not to touch me.

But my red silk
will lure the birds.
They'll eat me –

their beaks will tingle
their feathers tremble
as they feel my consciousness
            interrupt theirs.

The Voices

First, a sound from an animal
you can never imagine.

Then: insect-rustle, fish-hush.

And then the voices became louder.

Voice of an angel who is newly dead.
Voice of a child who refuses
to ever become an angel with wings.

Voice of tamarinds.
Voice of the colour blue.
Voice of the colour green.
Voice of the worms.
Voice of the white roses.
Voice of the leaves torn by goats.
Voice of the snake-pit.
Voice of the placenta.
Voice of the fetal heartbeat.
Voice of the scalped skull
whose hair hangs behind glass
in a museum.

I used to think there was
only one voice.
I used to wait
patiently for that one voice to return
to begin its dictation.

I was wrong.

I can never finish counting them now.
I can never finish
writing all they have to say.

Voice of the ghost who wants
to die again, but this time
in a brighter room with fragrant flowers

and different relatives.
Voice of the frozen lake.
Voice of the fog.
Voice of the air while it snows.
Voice of the girl
who still sees unicorns
and speaks to angels she knows by name.
Voice of pine tree sap.

And then the voices became louder.

Sometimes I hear them
laughing at my confusion.

And each voice insists
                and each voice knows
that it is the true one.

And each voice says: *follow me*
follow me and I will take you –

Notes

p.18 (Udaylee): untouchable when one is menstruating.

p.20 (Shérdi): sugar cane.

p.24 Sarasvati: the goddess of knowledge. She presides over all the Fine Arts and is worshipped in libraries.

p.32 The Gujarati is translated into English within the poem itself.

p.79 The quotation is the title poem from Pearse Hutchinson's collection, *The Soul that Kissed the Body* (Oldcastle, Co. Meath: The Gallery Press, 1990).

p.86 This poem refers to Pablo Picasso's painting, *Femme assise au chapeau poisson* (Sitting woman with fish hat), 1942.

p.89 Hanuman: the monkey god in Hindu mythology.

p.93 This poem refers to Edward Hopper's painting, *Rooms by the Sea*, 1951.

p.116 This poem refers to Georgia O'Keeffe's painting, *Cow's Skull – Red, White and Blue*, 1931.

p.117 All parts of 'Skinnydipping in History' in italics are quotations from John Ashbery's poems.

p.133 The epigraph of 'A Gujarati Patient Speaks' is a quotation from Otto Friedrich, *Glenn Gould: A Life and Variations* (Toronto: Lester & Orpen Dennys Ltd, 1989).

p.140 This poem partly addresses itself to a poem by Eleanor Wilner, 'Fears about the Moon', in her book *Otherwise* (Chicago: University of Chicago Press, 1993).